D0797116

Writing

BIOGRAPHY &
AUTOBIOGRAPHY

BRIAN D. OSBORNE

A & C Black • London

First published 2004
A & C Black Publishers Limited
37 Soho Square, London W1D 3QZ
www.acblack.com

ISBN 0–7136–6742–7

A CIP catalogue record for this book is
available from the British Library.

A & C Black uses paper produced with elemental chlorine-free pulp,
harvested from managed sustainable forests.

Typeset in 10.5/12.5pt Sabon
Printed and bound in Great Britain by
Creative Print and Design (Wales), Ebbw Vale

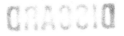

Contents

1

On Writing a Biography
or Autobiography

A rewarding undertaking

The aim of this book is quite simple. It is to help you write a biography or an autobiography. A biography is the story of a life, or of part of a life, told by someone other than the person concerned, while an autobiography is the story of one's own life. Most biographies focus on one person but can also be written about a couple, a family, or a group of people. Most of the advice in this book will be equally applicable to both biography and autobiography. Obviously, in the case of an autobiography you will be your own prime source of information – but you will still need to do research to fill in the context of your life, and you will still need to think about how best to present the unique wealth of information you possess.

While very few of us wake up one morning and think, 'I'll write a biography,' many people find themselves writing one almost without knowing it. You may have developed an interest in an institution – such as a parish church, a school or a factory – in a particular place or historic period, and have come across a character whose life-story could help to illuminate it. You might have been researching your family tree and been lucky enough to have found an ancestor with a particularly intriguing life, or for whom there are revealing and fascinating sources like a diary or account book or letters. You may feel that your own life, or a part of it, is worth recording, either for a general audience or for your own family and friends. Any or all of these things can start you off on the fascinating adventure that is writing biography. Never underestimate the importance of 'accident' in starting off a piece of biographical research.

However, be warned! Writing biography can become addictive – you might end up totally hooked, and start to eat, sleep and dream your subject. You will certainly run the very real risk of becoming a bore and find yourself telling all your friends more than they would ever want to know about your latest discoveries, or about the problems you are encountering in your research. Equally certainly, writing a biography brings it own rewards. You will enter into the life of your subject in a very exciting way. While you will never know all about them (even if the subject is yourself!), you will develop an understanding and a rapport with them that can be very satisfying and this can happen even if your subject is long dead. You will become an expert – even if in a very limited and narrow area – and this is always good for your self-esteem and your reputation. You will find fascinating connections between your subject and a host of other topics that would never have occurred to you before you became a biographer. You will certainly for ever after look at other biographies in quite a different light – analysing how the author has handled the sources, what these sources were, how they would have been used had you written the story, how the book has been structured, and a dozen other points of technique.

Writing biographies is fun. Sometimes, it can even be profitable – a point that I will return to later in this chapter. It must also be said that all too frequently, writing biographies can be frustrating, tedious, hard work that you will probably at some point regret starting and despair of finishing. However, if you persevere, the end result – which will never be perfect – will assuredly make up for all the hard work and frustration.

Avoiding the pitfalls

This book will share some ideas with you about how you might approach your biographical project, and share some experiences with you so you can avoid some of the pitfalls that await you. It will also point you in the direction of useful sources and techniques.

My qualification for writing this book is that I have done the job: I have written, and had published, three full-length biographies in addition to writing a lot of shorter biographical articles for magazines. In the course of doing so I have made lots of mistakes and learned many valuable lessons – the hard way. I am, of course, still making mistakes and learning lessons, because you never finish learning; nor do you ever reach some sort of 'biographer's paradise' where you find all the sources you need and everything is clear and straightforward. I hope that reading this book will assist you over or around some of the problems, and help you to bring your biographical project to a satisfactory conclusion.

Because every potential subject is different, this help and advice must inevitably be fairly general in its nature. As you would imagine, the documentary sources for a life of a 16th century poet are completely different from those for an 18th century soldier or a 20th century mill-worker. It is not possible to say that you will find the documents you want in this library, or in that record office; indeed, many of the people you might be interested in writing about will have left very little trace of their lives in documentary sources. Very often, the more 'ordinary' the subject, the more difficult it is to find evidence that they ever existed, let alone evidence of their political, religious or social views, their dress and appearance or the routine details of their daily life. It is however possible to use, with appropriate care, general sources such as parish registers, poor-law records and newspapers from which to extrapolate the life experience of individuals. There is also a common area of research technique and methodology, of construction and writing craft that can be applied to all forms of biographical writing.

The lack of detailed individual documentary sources is a rather discouraging thought and is particularly true for subjects from the earlier historic periods. However, it can also be surprisingly hard to uncover any personal information on even quite prominent figures, and from periods as well documented as the 18th century, for example. It then becomes much more difficult for you to get any real feel for their personality or their lifestyle – however comprehensively their professional career or land-holding, their births and deaths and marriages are documented. This should not prevent you from trying to work on such figures, because the situation with regard to archives and other sources is constantly changing and improving. A project that might have been hard to undertake satisfactorily a few years ago can often be much more easily carried out now.

Writing about real people

It seems to be a fundamental part of human nature to have a healthy interest in other people – in what motivates, inspires and drives them, and in the experiences that formed them. Equally we are all, to some extent, concerned to make sure that other people understand us; this can make us want to put our views 'on the record' – to tell something of our story in our own way, and leave behind some record of our being. The enormous explosion of interest in genealogy and family history in recent years testifies to this fascination with knowing who we are and where we come from.

Biography (or autobiography) is a very popular form of writing and has enjoyed this status for a long time. While telling tales about people must have been a part of human life since we learned to speak, the practice of writing comprehensive, analytical life-stories came into common use in Britain in the 18th century. Samuel Johnson's *Lives of the English Poets* (1779–81) broke new ground and Johnson himself became immortalised in what is often claimed as the greatest biography in the language: James Boswell's *The Life of Samuel Johnson* (1791). Boswell also has claims to fame as an autobiographer – his many volumes of journals (Yale University Press, 1950 onwards) are among the most frank and revealing accounts of one man's public, personal and inner life ever set down. They are certainly on a par with Samuel Pepys's diaries, and possibly more fascinating for having been a lifetime's preoccupation. Although not structured as an autobiography and not intended for publication in his own lifetime, Boswell's journals give a vivid picture of a remarkable man and a valuable insight into his times – and you cannot ask for more from an autobiography or a biography.

The interest in biography thus relates to a very basic human impulse. So basic and universal is this interest that everyone, to some extent, is a writer of biography (even if we hardly aspire to being a Pepys, a Boswell or a Dr Johnson!). The brief, photo-copied note about your family's experiences over the last year

4

sent out with the Christmas card is a sort of biography. The letter to a friend, catching up on news and gossip, is also a sort of biography. It may be one side of A4 paper rather than a 100,000-word text, but it is still the story of a life or lives recorded for others to read. Many writers of more formal biographies would be grateful for just such notes and letters as raw material for their work.

So biography and autobiography involve writing about real people, and they are not unique in this: fiction, in all its many forms, is also a people-centred form of writing. Much fiction is based on personal experience either modified or transformed by the novelist's imagination, so biography and fiction are often closer than practitioners of either genre find it comfortable to admit. Some, though not all, biography has definite elements of fiction in it – invented conversations, the exposition of a character's thought processes, descriptions of places and events where no contemporary record exists. This can be harmless. Indeed, at times, an imaginative leap based on a thorough knowledge of the period and topic can be enormously helpful – even, some would argue, essential – in filling-in undocumented periods and passages, and in explaining actions and motivations. As you work on the life of a subject, you will develop the sort of understanding of their character which allows you to make such imaginative leaps with reasonable assurance. If you know how your character responded to a particular situation on three documented occasions, then it would be fair to extrapolate from that how they might have reacted on a fourth occasion for which there is no documentary evidence. With time and study and prolonged exposure to your subject you will develop an increasingly clear idea of their thoughts and instincts and can make some appropriate deductions from this intimate knowledge.

However, there are dangers for the biographer in going too far beyond the sources and straying into the realm of fiction. Real people deserve respect. As a biographer, one of your responsibilities is to maintain your subject's intellectual integrity – in other words, to avoid attributing to them views or actions for which there is no evidence. Quoting conversations for which there is no possible evidence, or attributing states of mind for which there is no documentation, comes dangerously close to invention. It is possible to write gripping, psychologically insightful biography without having recourse to fiction, and the writer who respects the integrity of their subject and sources is more likely to be trusted when legitimate imaginative leaps are made.

Illuminating history

Biography is not history – or perhaps more exactly, history is not biography. The two disciplines of course have much in common and perhaps the distinctions are too easily made. Certainly Ralph Waldo Emerson, the 19th century American writer, suggested that 'There is properly no history, only biography'; while in one of his novels the 19th century British statesman Benjamin Disraeli declared: 'Read no history, nothing but biography, for that is life without theory.' A good biography will illuminate a historical period by focusing on the detail of life, manners, attitudes and beliefs in a way that many histories fail to do. Many biographies are really histories of a period, disguised as the story of a life, and are none the worse for that.

Sadly much contemporary historical writing, especially that coming from academic circles, is far from approachable and often seems to ignore the human dimension. Old-fashioned history – the type of writing that concentrated on the deeds of kings and great men to the exclusion of the life, concerns and activities of most of the rest of society – has rightly been overtaken by more rigorous and theoretical studies which look for wider socio-economic explanations, and by studies which reclaim from obscurity the experiences of the ordinary man and woman. The danger in this move away from the grand narrative is that increasingly, the historian will be writing for other historians and lose sight of the 'general reader'.

Biography can very usefully and conveniently bridge this gap. It can be thorough, rigorous, demanding in its use of and reliance on documented sources; but because it generally has a strong narrative drive and follows, however loosely, the events of a life, it retains human interest and the ability to appeal to a wider audience. Biographies such as Michael Holroyd's *Bernard Shaw* display a high level of scholarship and a mastery of source material which will meet the demands of academe but remain accessible to, and popular with, a wider audience. For many people it is probably easier to understand the British Civil Wars through a biography such as Antonia Fraser's *Cromwell, our Chief of Men*, than through reading any number of historical texts on the period. Of course you, as the biographer, have to master the historical texts and understand the historical context of your subject; but you can aim to make this research and learning palatable and attractive to a wider audience through your interpretative skills and your focus on an individual life. As the distinguished American historian Barbara Tuchman wrote:

> As a prism of history, biography attracts and holds the reader's interest in the larger subject. People are interested in other people, in the fortunes of the individual.
> ...biography is useful because it encompasses the universal in the particular. It is a focus that allows both the writer to narrow his field to manageable dimensions and the reader to more easily comprehend the subject.*

Because biography is fact-based it sometimes fails to get proper recognition as a form of creative writing. In reality, the skills of creative writing are just as much needed in the construction of a biography as they are in a novel, a short story, a poem or a play.

Story-telling skills are needed; the reader has to be drawn into your narrative, held by it for the duration of the story and delivered safely at the end, hopefully enriched or informed or amused. Like any other form of writing, a biography has to have a *shape* – a beginning, middle, and an end – and as I will suggest later, this need not slavishly follow the subject's life from cradle to grave. Just as variation of pace is needed in fiction, so it is with biography.

The importance of context

A particular challenge with biography, and especially with one set in a non-contemporary period, is ensuring that your reader has

*Tuchman, Barbara: *Biography as a Prism of History* in Pachter, Marc: *Telling Lives: the Biographer's Art*, New Republic Books, 1979

enough background information to put the events of your subject's life into some form of context. The pace of change in life today is such that almost any biography you write, or indeed any autobiography, will be set in a period that is unfamiliar in at least some respects to the intended readership. Biographies of current sport and pop stars are perhaps the only exception to this rule, but the life-story of a person now in their sixties will start during the Second World War, will span the era of food rationing, the age before mass foreign travel, before television, and take in memories of events such as the Korean War, the Suez Crisis, the Cuban Missile Crisis and the assassination of President Kennedy. These may be no more than vaguely understood concepts to a younger audience and may need to be explained.

This sort of explanation is essential both for your reader's understanding and enjoyment. A biography of a late 19th century British soldier needs to convey quite a lot of information about the British Army, international affairs, and the general social and economic history of the period in which he served. This information may appear rather dull, or at any rate, rather hard to make interesting. How it is to be conveyed, in what sized pieces, how soon in the narrative does your reader need to know it, how much can you assume of the general knowledge of your reader – these are all extremely tricky questions and are not the least of the challenges that the biographer faces.

An autobiography set during the Second World War probably does not need to explain to the reader who Adolf Hitler or Winston Churchill were, but the reader of our 19th century soldier's life might well need to have references to Bismarck and the Marquis of Salisbury explained, at least in broad detail – despite the fact that they occupied positions equivalent to those of Hitler and Churchill. Each project will present similar issues, and to give too much or too obvious information is likely to be as annoying and as off-putting to the reader as to give too little. The level at which you are writing has an enormous influence here: if you are targeting a specialist audience then you can probably safely assume that they will know enough of the background to make sense of your narrative. Certainly, they will not want to be fed a stream of totally redundant information, which could be seen as offensively patronising. If you are aiming at a more general readership then you may very well have to go a bit further down the explanatory path. Perhaps it might be useful to give some thought to finding a way of structuring this necessary information so that the reader who needs it can find it, while the reader who doesn't need it can skip it – an obviously titled preliminary chapter, or an appendix, might be a way of dealing with this.

In one of my own biographies I was faced with just this problem. I was writing about an 18th century Scottish lawyer and judge, Lord Braxfield – a man with a very dark and sinister reputation. I felt that before I could take the reader through the events of Braxfield's life I had three preliminary issues to address. The first was a discussion of the sources of this reputation (I hoped that by the end of the book, readers might be able to judge for themselves its validity); the second was a description of Scotland and Scottish society in the 18th century; and the third, and perhaps the most difficult area for the non-specialist reader, was an account of the Scottish legal system. Once I had got these out of the way I felt that the reader and I could go on our journey through Braxfield's life on fairly equal terms and the narrative need not be interrupted by too frequent explanations of unfamiliar terms or concepts. Of course, such a strategy has its dangers. One reviewer of my book remarked that I had little that was novel to say about Scottish history and the Scottish legal system, and that my approach was rather naïve; while another reviewer praised the book for giving a splendid account of the state of Scotland's law and institutions. To the first comment, I can only plead guilty, and argue in my defence that my potential non-specialist readers might possibly benefit more from a naïve overview than from a penetrating, groundbreaking and possibly unintelligible analysis. To the second comment I can only say, thank you!

The necessary skills

There are shelves and shelves of biographies of people like Mary, Queen of Scots, Admiral Nelson and Queen Victoria. The details of their lives are well known, and it will not come as a surprise to the reader of the latest biography of Nelson that he dies at Trafalgar in 1805 or that Mary has her head chopped off at Fotheringay Castle in 1587. Why, then, do new biographies of extremely famous and well-documented characters keep getting written, published and read?

One obvious answer is that such books sell. But on another level, the justification for the appearance of yet another biography of Queen Victoria is seldom to be found in new facts or new sources. The more usual explanation is that the author has found a new approach or a new interpretation, or has re-told what is a familiar enough story in a new and exciting way. The latest biography of Nelson is thus more likely to be justified by the author's writing skills and imagination than by their research skills. An author could be lucky and amazingly industrious, and find extensive new sources – but if this industry and luck is not allied to perception and to basic written communication skills they will be of little avail. A good biographer needs the same qualities that go to make a good novelist or a good playwright. Characters need to be made to live. Locations need to be vividly portrayed. Writing needs to have pace and variety and colour.

Of course, there are skills particular to the biographer: a sense of what makes the past different from the present, a sensitivity to changing social and moral values, an ear for the changing patterns of language and an appreciation of changing usages are all key attributes. Let us take just one simple example, concerning letter-writing. Today when we write to people we have never met or spoken to, even on business matters, we often use a personal and informal form of address – 'Dear Brian'. Not so very many years ago, people who had known each other for years and were on friendly terms quite naturally wrote to each other and addressed their letters using only their correspondent's last name. One might construct a hierarchy of forms of address that would have been understood and practised by many people during much of the 19th and 20th centuries:

- The most formal – Dear Sir
- Less formal – Dear Mr Osborne
- A more friendly form used among equals – Dear Osborne
- An even more intimate form – My Dear Osborne

The use of the Christian name would have been reserved for

family and the closest of friends. If you are not aware of this changing social custom it can be quite easy to misinterpret the tone of a letter.

The documents that you will use to research your biography were not, except in a very few cases, written so that you could write a biography. While you may be lucky enough to find a memoir or an account of a life, which was deliberately written for posterity, more frequently you will be scanning documents created for entirely different purposes and desperately trying to extract every last drop of the information you want from them. This process can be far from easy. Let us leave aside the complexities of reading a document written many centuries ago in an unfamiliar hand or in a foreign language, and concentrate on documents that do not present such difficulties. There is the basic problem of understanding the document. Can you work out what all the words mean? When people wrote to each other or filled in forms they frequently used shortcuts, abbreviations and colloquialisms – just as we do. Some are reasonably familiar, such as the annotation on a Census return of 'ag. lab.' for Agricultural Labourer, or 'HLW' for Hand Loom Weaver. Others are far more obscure and will require a better knowledge of the period or the place to interpret.

Words do not always have the obvious meaning that we might imagine them to have. I examined a Scottish will from the late 19th century which left money to a church and made reference to 'Fencing the Table'. This was not a reference to a physical fence but to the practice of examining those seeking to take Holy Communion and excluding those who were considered unworthy. The biographer must of course develop the skill of interpreting these words and phrases, but should first be alert enough to recognise that there is in fact a problem – that the words may not mean what they appear to mean on the surface, or that a 21st century interpretation of them may not be correct. Words and phrases not only fall into disuse, but also change their meaning over time, so you need to be sure of the sense in which they were being used in your source document. In Chapter 6 we will look at some of the tools you can use to help in this, but it is worth remembering that although the dictionary may correctly state that by, say, the mid-18th century a word had taken on a certain meaning, the person who actually wrote that word in the mid-18th century might have been old, a traditionalist, living in a part of the country where an older usage had survived, or simply seeking after an effect and so quite deliberately using the word in an archaic sense. This might seem like a fairly hopeless problem but, with luck and experience, you will get a feel for people in the past and become fairly confident about interpreting them.

Managing the matters of truth and objectivity

Just as you need to remember that letters, reports, census forms, legal documents and so forth were not created simply for our convenience, so you also need to remember that what is written in them may not be true.

Historians and biographers place great emphasis on distinguishing between 'primary' and 'secondary' sources. In essence, a primary source is a document written at the time to which it refers – a census return, a diary, a letter, a tax-form; while a secondary source is an interpretation of history – a newspaper, a history book, another biography. A secondary source may be contemporary with the event it describes or it may be much later, and there are clearly gradations of value in secondary sources. For example, one would normally place more reliance on information in a scholarly textbook than on a weekly magazine article, or take a report in a broadsheet newspaper more seriously than one in a popular tabloid.

This is a valuable distinction, and where possible and practical one should certainly always try to go back to primary sources. But primary sources are not infallible. They may have been written with partial knowledge. They may have been written to put the best possible interpretation on the author's actions. They may indeed have been written deliberately with the intent of deceiving. An entry I found in the 1841 British Census had a woman's age given as 58. From other sources I knew that she was in fact 71 at that time. By the 1851 census the same lady was giving her age as 72, when of course she had reached the age of 81. She died in 1856 at the age of 85, so we do not know what story she would have told the 1861 Census! The biographer needs to develop a profound scepticism, to take nothing on trust. Always ask yourself why a document was written, why it says what it says, whether its statements are internally consistent and whether they can be backed up by other sources. In the Census example I mentioned there is in fact another problem: the rules for the 1841 Census dictated that for those aged more than 15, the return should round down to the nearest five years. The enumerator who recorded the lady's age as 58 was actually making an error, so we have a doubly erroneous primary source – one of the errors appearing to be a woman being coy about her age, and the other an enumerator failing to follow instructions.

Not all unreliable primary sources are deliberately false, of course. Sometimes genuine ignorance on the part of the writer or compiler means that they give wrong information. A particular difficulty in dealing with any time before the 20th century is making allowance for the slowness of communications. You need to have a rough idea of how long it took letters to travel from one place to another.

The novelist L P Hartley wrote in *The Go-Between*: 'The past is a foreign country: they do things differently there.' This is a great and important truth, awareness of which should always be with us when writing biographies; and making proper allowance for that truth is one of the core skills that the biographer has to learn. It is not just a question of grappling with the technicalities, such as how long it took a letter to go from London to York in 1700, or what 'nice' meant in 1650, or what the SPCK was. Through time, life's moral and ethical dimensions change, and the biographer – while not being required to abandon 21st century morality, ethics or religion – has to appreciate that in the past, perfectly decent people could support views or advocate policies which to most people today seem outrageous or evil.

Slavery, for example, was for centuries a perfectly normal part of life and commerce. People who considered themselves, and were considered by their contemporaries, to be good, decent and virtuous profited from it. As we are well aware, large parts of British industry and commerce, to say nothing of the British Empire, were built on it. Looking back, few of us today would dispute that slavery was wrong, and indeed there were always people morally opposed to it; but because an 18th century person profited from the slave trade is in itself no reason for the 21st century biographer to attribute immorality or hypocrisy to their subject.

On a less extreme level it was considered perfectly normal in the 18th and 19th centuries for political influence to be used in a way that, to our modern eyes, seems highly improper. This found its expression both in small things and in larger matters. Before the advent of the penny post, British mail services were extremely expensive. People in official positions, such as Members of Parliament, had the privilege of franking mail to send it free of charge and extended this privilege to friends for use on non-official correspondence. Appointments to office went as often by connection and cronyship as by merit. It was an accepted part of life that if you wished a post in the Civil Service you sought a well-placed, politically active sponsor.

If there is a requirement for the biographer to be sensitive to changes over time, and not to look at the past through modern eyes only, then there is also a requirement for the biographer to look at their own prejudices and preconceptions. There is of course a place for subjective, even deliberately unobjective, polemical biography. Lytton Strachey's famous demolition of some 19th century historical characters in *Eminent Victorians* (1918) is a prime example of the value and merit of such a process, and one can hardly object to it when it is presented in such an open way. What is more worrying is the apparently objective biography, which is written with an ulterior motive or to promote a political or ideological viewpoint and which attempts to conceal its lack of objectivity.

Now objectivity may be an unreachable goal. It is extremely hard to 'get outside' your own preconceptions and prejudices and be truly objective, but it is essential for the biographer to be aware of those prejudices and perhaps seek to compensate for them.

No biography is, or can be, the full, unvarnished story of a life. This would take a library full of books to record, would take longer to read than to live and would be monumentally boring: 'Robert went to bed and enjoyed six-and-a-half hours' unbroken sleep.' Our job as biographers or autobiographers is to select, to condense, to simplify, to draw inferences and conclusions – and, I would suggest, to present the evidence to our readers in as open and fair a way as possible. Of course this is not easy. As soon as we start to select we introduce our own minds, personalities and prejudices into the equation:

- I think this fact is less important than that.
- I think this letter need not be quoted.
- I think an extract from this document will be sufficient.
- I think if I summarise this argument in this way, that will be adequate.
- I think that if I introduce this idea here it is better than introducing it there.
- I will describe this character in these terms rather than in some other way.

Being selective is inevitable and necessary – but we need to be aware that we are doing it, that there are other options, and that the way we have chosen owes everything to our characters, our background, experience, education and formation.

There is a couplet from Rudyard Kipling's poem *In the Neolithic Age*:

There are nine and sixty ways of constructing tribal lays
And – every – single – one – of – them – is – right!

There are certainly just as many ways of constructing biographies. Whether they can all be right is certainly an interesting thought, but one which need not detain us now; what is important is that we remember that there are always other ways of presenting the information we have gathered. Our choices are not necessarily 'right', nor are they ruled by some objective truth like a law of physics.

The nature of your subject will of course have a huge impact on this question of objectivity. Can you be really objective if you are writing about Adolf Hitler? Can you be objective, from the other direction, if you are writing the life of a Saint or of a character whom you have always admired? Of course, most of our biographical subjects fall somewhere in the middle range of humanity – somewhere between the extremes of St Francis of Assisi and Hitler – but even so, they may present some problems. Do you allow yourself to be judgemental or do you present the evidence and let the reader decide? If the latter, be aware that your selection and presentation of the evidence is inevitably going to be coloured by your own views and background. If you try your best to be even-handed and fair, and conscientiously attempt to show your subject as a man or woman of their time burdened with all the intellectual and social baggage of their age, rather than as an unmitigated villain or a total saint, you will probably be accused of rehabilitating them on one hand or denigrating them on the other. Nobody said that writing biography was easy!

In *Truth to Life: the Art of Biography in the Nineteenth Century*, A O J Cockshut says that the biographer has to:

> ... submit his interpretations to the pressure of facts. The difficulty of biography as an art lies mainly in this tension between interpretation and evidence ...

and he goes on to note that:
> ... a batch of letters and dates is not a biography. Books written by authors who were uncertain of what they really thought of their subjects, or afraid to say, are quickly forgotten.*

Biographers are sometimes said to fall in love with their subjects. This may be a slightly exaggerated statement but there is quite clearly a temptation to become 'uncritical', because you have got to know and perhaps understand somebody, and maybe feel that you know them better than anyone else. This is probably as dangerous and certainly as unsatisfactory as the 'knocking' type of biography.

The type of biography or autobiography that you are writing has a major effect on all these questions of balance and objectivity, of truth and interpretation. A brief article for a popular magazine must inevitably shortcut some of the issues, because of its readership and the constraints of space. Rather than laying out a chain of evidence and discussing the interpretation of the evidence, as one would reasonably be required to do in a full-

*Cockshut, A O J: *Truth to Life: the Art of Biography in the Nineteenth Century*, Collins, 1974

length book or in an essay for a learned journal, authors are probably expected (and can probably afford) to be much more direct and judgemental – while, of course, remaining true to the essential facts and to their view of the character. A biography written for children might properly simplify, but hopefully not distort, the issues. The degree of simplification that was felt necessary would of course depend on the age group for which the biography was intended.

So, having looked at some of the basic issues in writing biography – and we will return to a number of them later in this book – what form will your biography or autobiography take?

Commercial publication – books and periodicals

The traditional form of the biography is as a commercially produced book – the form that runs from Boswell's *Johnson* through Holroyd's *Shaw* to the latest biography of the action-packed life of a 23-year-old footballer. There was in the 19th century a huge outpouring of very long biographies, often called something like *The Life and Letters of ...* These tended to be dull, formal and uncritical and were in fact often written by people who had some form of loyalty to their subject – such as the standard life of the Prime Minister William Gladstone, which was written by John Morley who had been one of Gladstone's cabinet ministers. Some were masterpieces, though – Lockhart's multi-volume life of his father-in-law Sir Walter Scott being a prime example. It was however against the flood of Victorian hagiography that Lytton Strachey reacted in *Eminent Victorians* – although Strachey replaced one sort of prejudice with another.

These massive Victorian biographies have become the quarries from which later writers have formed their own interpretations. Writing of Strachey's life of Florence Nightingale, and of the 19th century life of Nightingale by Cook, Milicent Bell observed:

Most biographers since Cook – like Cecil Woodham-Smith

– have simply based their accounts on Cook's basic research, and Strachey, of course, never looked at a document; he had only his intuitions.*

Closer to our own day, biography has tended to be more analytical, more psychological, although there is still a huge demand for the simpler story of an interesting life, well told. Biographies of one sort or another are published in considerable quantity. In the year 2000, of the 116,415 new titles published in the UK, 3114** fell into the category of biography; and this number could even understate the biographical output, as some books that fall into other categories might have a strong biographical element. As encouraging for the potential biographer or autobiographer is the fact that sales of such books are very substantial. Almost 1.9 million copies of biographies with a total value of £21.6 million, and 4.6 million copies of autobiographies with a total value of £47.4 million, were recorded in the year 2000.***

Many of us would be daunted by the prospect of starting work on a major biography of a major figure – Bernard Shaw, or Winston Churchill for example – not least at the thought of the mass of documents that would have to be mastered. While writing biographies without adequate archive materials is difficult, the problems of dealing with the life of a copiously documented character like Shaw or Churchill are just as real, and the skills involved in mastering them should not be underestimated. Simply handling the mass of documents generated by such a life, and organising this information (see also Chapter 7), is a formidable task – as is getting to grips with your subject's background so that you can recognise, and interpret for your reader, allusions to contemporary concerns, people and events.

However, the first-time biographer is unlikely to become the official biographer of a great statesman or a major literary celebrity. Indeed, the first-time biographer is more likely not to start with a book at all. There is a huge range of periodicals that offer us opportunities for the publication of biographical material. Few, if any, specialise in biographical writing but many do

*Bell, Milicent: *Lytton Strachey's Eminent Victorians* in Meyers, Jeffrey: *The Biographer's Art*, Macmillan, 1988
**Whitaker Information Services
***Whitaker Book Track

carry some biographical content. Magazines – ranging from the international such as *Readers' Digest*, through UK titles to periodicals of more local scope such as *The Scots Magazine* or *Staffordshire Life* – all present opportunities to place biographical articles. In Chapter 11 we will look at the requirements and demands of such publications; sufficient for now to note that a large market exists and needs to be supplied. In addition to these general-interest and geographically focused magazines there exists a bewildering array of specialist periodicals that are also possible outlets for biographical articles. A glance at the shelves of a well-stocked newsagent will provide many fruitful ideas.

Non-commercial writing – self- and vanity publishing

'No man, but a blockhead, ever wrote, except for money' – or so thought Dr Samuel Johnson. Well, I suppose I must be counted a blockhead because, although I very much like getting paid for writing, I have actually been known to write without any financial reward. Some books and periodicals are clearly non-commercial, usually because they are so specialised, or so limited in circulation, that it would be impossible to produce them if the contributors had to be paid. If there is no financial reward then there is usually another sort of reward – perhaps the satisfaction of helping a society or an institution that you are associated with, or local loyalty in contributing to the publication of a book or periodical centred on your home area, or simply the pleasure of seeing somebody in whom you have become interested gain recognition through your writing.

It must be acknowledged that some publishers do take advantage of authors eager to be published, and offer no payment. This is particularly true in the academic field, where authors are so driven by the need to publish that they accept, both in periodical and in book form, a situation where either no payment or a merely nominal payment is made. Sadly this practice shows signs of spilling over from academic publishing and affecting potentially commercial areas, and should be resisted. However, there are times when 'writing for love' is appropriate and of course a publication record, even in such unremunerative outlets, can be very helpful when you are trying to interest a more commercially orientated publisher in a project. A list of publication credits and evidence that other people have found your work acceptable can be a great help in establishing your credentials as a good risk, and as a competent writer who can deliver the goods.

You may not even seek to have your work commercially produced. This is often the case with autobiographical projects: perhaps you only want to produce a few copies of your memoirs for your friends and families, or you are doubtful about how many people would really want to read your recollections of being evacuated during the Second World War or your memories of life in the cotton-mills. Not so long ago a writer in such a situation had very few options. The book could be produced as a typescript, photocopied, perhaps bound; but many writers felt that they wanted something better and more impressive, and followed up advertisements from what have become known as 'vanity publishers'. These are firms which, for a fee – usually a very substantial fee – will take your manuscript and produce it as a 'proper' book. However, they are likely to make very little effort on the editorial, production or sales fronts, and their interest in the title generally terminates when your cheque clears. The products of such vanity publishers are seldom reviewed in the press; they seldom win a place on bookshop shelves; and the end result is that the author winds up with a garage full of books that nobody wants to buy. Vanity publishing is not necessarily a bad thing, but an author who chooses to go down that route has to accept that it is a very expensive process – and that it is in the highest degree unlikely that their money will be recouped. If you want to see your work in print, and have no concerns about the cost, well and good.

With the advent of computer technology, self-publishing has become much more practical, and short print-runs are no longer necessarily a recipe for financial disaster and unbearable unit costs. The essence of self-publishing is that you take all the financial risk (and of course reap all the financial benefits), arranging all the processes from origination, design, art-work, printing, binding, through to sales and distribution. If you wish to make a financial success of self-publishing you will have an enormous amount of hard work to face – work which may not be all to your taste. Yes, it can be enjoyable to discuss with a designer or a printer exactly how your book should look, and you will have much more artistic control over the process than any commercial publisher will allow you; but you will also have to take on the potentially heart-breaking task of selling your book to bookshops and other outlets. With your inevitable emotional commitment to the book, a refusal to stock it will be felt as a rejection of you, your work and even your whole being. You will also have to deal with the less than exciting business of invoicing, packing and dispatch, and the very troublesome business of getting your bills paid. Bookshops may insist on sale-or-return terms and will look for long periods of credit: 30 days, 60 days, or even more. Self-publishing can be, and has been, done with great success – but nobody who has done it would claim that it is an easy option.

Web publishing

The other non-commercial outlet for your work, and one with much less financial outlay, is web publishing – putting your work out there on the Internet. This need cost little or nothing: if you have an email provider such as Freeserve or BT Openworld, the Information Service Provider (ISP) will generally include in the package something like 30 to 50 megabytes of web space free of charge. This is more than ample to host a very substantial work, complete with illustrations.

The process of creating a website is covered in many books and magazines. For our purposes at this time it is sufficient to say that web publishing offers many advantages – and of course, a few disadvantages:

- Very significantly, the creator has complete control over how the material appears. For example, in conventional publishing your book publisher may feel unwilling to use more than, say, 20 illustrations – but on the Internet, although pictures take up more bytes of space than words, you can include all the illustrations you think desirable. You can even, again at a space cost, include sound or moving pictures to illustrate and enhance your text.
- Web publishing is not simply an electronic version of ink-on-

paper publishing. It offers the opportunity to do things that a book cannot do. You can develop interactivity and feedback facilities – ask your reader what they think, find out if they have more information, enter into discussion and debate with them through message boards and similar devices.

- Web publishing enables you to move away from the linear nature of the book – one page following another, one fact following another – and perhaps construct a biography that more accurately represents real life than the sometimes artificial hierarchy imposed by print media.
- Web publishing is fluid. When a book is conventionally published it is fixed – of course, a new edition can be produced, but 2000 or 20,000 copies have been printed and have to be sold. The day after the book is printed you discover a new and interesting fact, or a document suddenly turns up and you can do nothing about it. By contrast your website can be continuously revised and brought up to date, and can always represent the best version of your story, or the most accurate account of your thoughts and opinions.

Of course there is a major downside to web publishing: your website only exists for as long as you are using that particular ISP. If they go out of business, or you stop your subscription to them, then your website is no more! While you can archive it on your computer and re-mount it on a new ISP's site, this hardly makes for easy accessibility.

While your website may be interesting and popular, and receive lots of visits ('hits' in computer-speak), you will not make any money from it and you may find that your copyright – your intellectual property rights – are not respected. Other people may feel themselves free to make use of your material, sometimes in ways you disapprove of, and frequently without proper attribution. We will look more at the question of copyright as it affects the writer in Chapter 9, but it can be said now that the Internet is still a jungle where copyright is concerned. Because of this, a conventional publisher may have doubts about publishing your book if it has already been released on the Internet. Conversely, there are obvious marketing advantages to having samples of a traditionally published book available on a website – sufficient to give a taste of the whole, and hopefully to attract

Internet surfers to buy the book.

A more sophisticated computer-based delivery system is now attracting attention: the e-book. Unlike the website publishing concept, which is open to both amateur and institutional publishers, the e-book is a commercially driven system of publishing designed to be read on computer screen – either your domestic desktop or laptop, or the Pocket Digital Assistants (PDAs) which are gaining in popularity as notebooks/address books/diaries. E-books are delivered by means of a variety of software packages and some commercial publishers are investing heavily in this type of venture. Whether anyone really wants to read a full-length book on a hand-held PDA, or even sitting in front of a desktop computer, is however something of an open question.

2

Can Anyone Do It?

Experts versus 'amateurs'

The obvious answer to the question of 'who should write biographies' (or autobiographies) might seem to be: 'Someone who knows all there is to know about the subject of the biography, and who is completely familiar with the background to their life.' However, this is not necessarily the complete answer, the only answer, or even, surprisingly enough, necessarily the best answer.

A better answer might be: 'Anyone who really wants to!' This is not to suggest that writing biographies is easy, but rather that it is what the author brings to the project, and the skills, insights and knowledge developed during the project, that count. For this very reason it is wise to do some research into your proposed subject before you get too committed to the project. You need to ensure that you have, or have access to, the specific skills that you might need to complete it successfully. If you do not read Italian fluently or cannot understand astrophysics, can you find a source of expertise or will your lack of knowledge compromise the project and, as importantly, frustrate and disappoint you?

Of course, many fine biographies are written by experts; but equally good biographies have been written by authors who were far from being experts when they started out, and who became a lot more expert in the course of writing their book. In effect the biography becomes a record of the author's discovery and exploration of the subject.

In some cases this has been taken even further, so that the biography has been transmuted into a record of the process – of the search for the subject. Two classic examples of this are A J A Symons's *The Quest for Corvo*, an enthralling story of the author's search for the truth about Frederick William Rolfe – the self-styled Baron Corvo, an enigmatic writer and aspirant to the priesthood; and a more recent work in the same vein, Ian Hamilton's *In Search of J D Salinger* – the fascinating story of Hamilton's attempt to write the biography of the reclusive American author of *Catcher in the Rye*. Both these books are eminently worth reading by anyone interested in the field of biography, and will surely raise many questions about the process of writing biography and the principles that underpin it.

Communicating your enthusiasm

It is all too easy to be put off the idea of writing a biography because you feel unequipped to do justice to the subject. An expert knowledge of the subject is enormously helpful and it would be foolish to argue otherwise. I referred in Chapter 1 to my own work on the Scottish judge, Lord Braxfield. I started on that project with very little knowledge of Scots law; and while I perhaps ended it with just a little more knowledge than I had when I began, I would, in many respects, have found it much easier to write had I been a 'proper' legal historian. My choice of the subject and my approach to the book came from a fascination with the image and character of the man rather than any detailed knowledge of 18th century Scots law and politics. I hope that my interest in the character and the strength of the story I had to tell transcended any of the technical difficulties of communicating the concepts and terms of Scots law.

The obvious danger in this type of 'amateur' (to use the word in its best sense) biography writing is that you will not always know where the pitfalls are. You may check all the references and read all the sources but, because of your lack of background, you can fail to see something very obvious that a trained expert would spot at once. Of course there are ways around this problem. For one thing, experts are frequently very willing to share their expertise and to look over your text and spot any blunders.

However, I think it can be argued that in writing for a general audience it is perfectly possible to produce a satisfactory result without having access to a great body of pre-existing expertise.

One could go even further and say that the general reader is quite often better served by the less-expert author – simply because the less-expert author is likely to be more attuned to the general reader's level of knowledge than is the expert. We have all met experts who are incapable of communicating their expertise to the man in the street; and we have all met the natural communicator who can take a subject and make it live and understood by a wide audience. In a way it is rather like the difference between a primary school teacher who has to teach 25 seven-year-olds everything from English and Maths to History and Science, and the university lecturer whose teaching is confined within a narrow, though high-level, specialisation. There are bad and good examples of both, and there is little doubt that if the specialist can communicate effectively then the end product will be better. If not, then the end product will inevitably address a limited and specialised market and the general reader will be frozen out. It is also true to say that all too often, experts do not see as part of their role the interpretation of their subject for the general, lay reader – which is unfortunate, but which does leave a wide field of writing activity open to the rest of us.

Seeing the bigger picture

The academic expert is likely to be focused on a fairly narrow field, whereas a generalist biographer like Antonia Fraser has written across a wide historical sweep where one would assume that there has been little opportunity for the transferability of specialist subject knowledge. Mary Queen of Scots (late 16th century), Cromwell (mid-17th century) and Marie Antoinette (late 18th century) represent just three of her major works. An academic historian might feel constrained by the period of their specialisation, but the non-academic biographer enjoys a greater freedom.

If as an 'amateur' or 'generalist' you follow up an interest and start writing a biography of, say, a 19th century Lancashire cotton-mill owner, you should recognise that, as a non-academic, you probably will never have the detailed knowledge of the 19th century Lancashire cotton trade and its socio-economic background possessed by an economic historian who has specialised in the subject. However, what you may well have, at the end of your journey through the project, is a far greater knowledge of that mill-owner, or that mill, or that mill community than anyone else – including the expert economic historian.

What is vital, and where the real problem for the generalist and amateur or 'one-off' biographer lies, is putting the local and the specific into its regional, national and international setting. Academic experts come to their specialised fields with the benefit of training in wider disciplines, and have learned to look for the broader picture – to find the significance of the local in the context of a broader canvas. If all your knowledge of the 19th century Lancashire cotton industry is confined to one mill, in one town, it becomes very difficult to decide whether something is important or unusual, and whether a process or a development was significant or just commonplace. This problem does not just affect the biographer. Local histories are very often flawed by their authors' inability to move from writing a chronicle of events in one town or village to communicating to the reader the story of how that town or village is typical or atypical, and showing what it has to say about wider themes and over-arching developments.

This is a problem, but fortunately it is a problem with a fairly obvious solution: reading. Read around your subject, read other books on related subjects, read other books about the same subject, read the specialists, and search out the places where research on your subject is being published – which may be in periodicals rather than in books. Advice on carrying out this research is given in Chapter 6. You may be surprised to discover just how much has already been written on your subject or on closely related topics – and indeed you may be slightly alarmed by the wealth of established academic expertise your reading reveals. There is no reason for this to put you off your project.

Despite the fact that you may find a great deal of academic research on a wide variety of subjects, this may be less of a competitive threat than you might think. It is a curious fact that in the United Kingdom today, the writing of biographies tends not to be done by academics. Michael Holroyd, the biographer of Shaw, Lytton Strachey and Augustus John, has pointed out that modern British biographers have usually been what he delightfully calls 'a maverick crew of self-employed writers unattached to universities'.* He distinguishes this situation from that prevailing in the United States, where he points out that biographers have more frequently been academics. Holroyd himself is a living demonstration of this tendency: not only does he not teach at a university, but he never attended one as an undergraduate, and he describes himself as being 'educated at Eton College and Maidstone Public Library'.

The reluctance of academics to write biography may have a number of explanations. There is certainly a view that biography is not a sufficiently rigorous academic discipline, and that it can all too easily become a theory-free zone that descends into simple story-telling. History, as we noted in Chapter 1, looks for broad socio-economic movements, theories and ideologies, and people regard with a certain degree of suspicion the story of an individual as a legitimate form of historical scholarship. However, there is some evidence of this situation changing with the appointment of Britain's first Professor of Biography, Nigel Hamilton, at De Montford University. And whatever the merits of this view, the positive result for the potential writer of biographies is that the field has been left open for other people to fill the gap.

Keeping some critical detachment

To be driven to write a biography by your own enthusiasm for the subject is often an enormous advantage, because it then becomes so much easier to win the interest of your potential readers. Enthusiasm is an infectious quality, without which it is very unlikely that you will be able to interest anyone else in the subject or communicate effectively with your potential readership. Enthusiasm is not, of course, the same thing as uncritical partisanship – which is as dangerous as naked hostility. You should be able to look at the subject of your biography with some degree of critical detachment, but you surely need to feel that their life is a story worth telling before you start on the very substantial amount of work involved. For my own part, there are many people who simply do not interest me as potential

*Library Association Record, March 2002

biographical subjects. This is true even of people who are quite close to subjects I have previously worked on, and who would thus be convenient and time-saving to research, because I could bring background knowledge of the period and sources to the project. Were I to write their lives, I am sure that my lack of interest and my resultant lack of emotional commitment would become all too apparent to the reader.

While lack of interest in a subject leads to the danger of hack work, a positive antipathy to a person is probably a useful indication that you should not be thinking of writing their biography – or at least that you should be giving very careful thought to the project. The objectivity and detachment required for good work are going to be so much more difficult to attain if everything about the subject of your book is distasteful to you. Of course, there have been excellent biographies written of subjects who must have been totally unsympathetic to the authors – Allan Bullock's much-praised *Hitler: a Study in Tyranny* comes to mind – but the selection of such a subject is probably not, for most of us, a very wise one for a first biography. Better by far for the first-time biographer to find a subject who offers slightly more opportunity for enthusiasm and commitment.

Of course there are two categories of subject where this problem of enthusiasm versus objectivity is particularly acute. Never having attempted to write my own life-story, I am not sure how one tackles the problem of objectivity in the autobiography! The words of Robert Burns come to mind:

Oh wad some Pow'r the giftie gie us
To see oorsels as others see us!
It wad frae mony a blunder free us,
And foolish notion.

I suspect that most people reading an autobiography do not really expect objectivity and detachment, and it must be said that they are not usually disappointed. An autobiography is so excellent an opportunity to put the writer's version of events on record that it can hardly be wondered that most autobiographers seize the opportunity with eager hands and present their story in their way, and usually to their advantage. For evidence, look at almost any ex-cabinet minister's memoirs.

The biography of a close friend or family member opens up another interesting set of problems. The biographer is in this case, by definition, an expert in their subject; they are also, by definition, committed, partial and prejudiced. This can make for great biography or for the distasteful settling of accounts. Boswell's *Johnson* and Lockhart's *Scott* provide classic examples of the former – and any number of 'kiss and tell' or 'my mother was a monster' showbusiness biographies provide vivid, if somewhat less edifying, examples of the latter.

Assuming that you are not writing an autobiography or the biography of a family member, then one of the great joys of being a biographer is that one can pick and chose whom you want to write about and, indeed, how you want to write about them. Of course, you may find that the subject or the approach that interests you does not work commercially – nobody may want to publish your book or article. However, you may feel that the process of researching and writing is satisfaction enough and of course one should never give up hope of finding a publisher. The most apparently *recherché* subjects can prove to be more than saleable. Who would have thought that the story of a little-known 18th century English clockmaker would have become an international bestseller and a TV movie ... but that is what happened to Dava Sobel's *Longitude*.

3

Why Write Biographies?

In one sense the answer is obvious. The main reason why many, or perhaps even most, people write biographies is to tell a life-story. However, it is worth bearing in mind that the biographical format is a very adaptable one which can be varied to suit a number of purposes.

Like most authors, biographers tend to write for their own pleasure and to satisfy their own interests, but they also need to have a thought to the requirements of their readers – at least when writing for the commercial sector. Authors and readers come to biographies for a variety of reasons: to understand someone better; to explore a period of time or a place or a subject area; or, in the case of autobiography, to validate their own life or to set down their own views. While most people will read what might be described as the 'traditional lives' – books like Elizabeth Longford's *Wellington* or Roy Jenkins's *Churchill* – and while these are the staples of the bookshop and library, the other functions of biography are worth considering briefly. Apart from telling the story of a famous life or lives, there are perhaps five other areas where the biographical format can be used.

Illustrating a subject area

The first of these is biography as an approach route to a subject area. For example, reading any one of the several lives of Thomas Telford (1757–1834) will give you, in a fairly painless and accessible manner, a considerable amount of information about 18th and 19th century civil engineering, road and bridge building. Reading a biography of Field Marshal Montgomery should leave you much better informed about military matters during the Second World War. Of course, all biographies are rooted in their subject's career or social circumstances and, apart from those rather rare works which focus entirely on an inner life, must inevitably convey some information about the life's setting. There are however people who might not be a Telford or a Montgomery, and may not be thought to be sufficiently interesting or famous to warrant a biography, but because of their involvement with a significant area at a key moment in time can become symbolic representations of that area. As a result one often reads their story less out of an interest in the individual life-experience than as an accessible way into an understanding of the subject area. The memoirs of Benjamin Harris – an apparently unremarkable private soldier in the British Army during the Napoleonic Wars – were published as *The Recollections of Rifleman Harris*, and provide a unique account of the Peninsular Campaign from the perspective of the rank-and-file soldier. Such a perspective would be far less evident in a standard military history or in the biography of a great general like Wellington.

There are a number of issues to be considered if you are a biographer contemplating this approach. One is unfortunately commercial: will a publisher be interested in your groundbreaking life of Ebenezer Brown, the pioneer of modern pig husbandry? Having to finance projects with their own money, publishers are naturally cautious, and the idea of bringing out the 'first ever' book on a particular subject is not always as appealing to them as its author might think. Authors can be, at times, rather naïve about this – I certainly was when I wrote my first biography, which I now realise was very much a 'life as a contribution to a subject area' type of book. My 'life' was Henry Bell and the subject area was the development of steam navigation in Britain. There had been no biography of Bell since the publication of a rather unsatisfactory one in 1844, and I thought that after 150 years the world was ready for a better one. As there was no competitive work on the market I even allowed myself to entertain fond delusions that publishers would be keen to fill this subject gap and would rush to accept my book. The 19 who rejected it obviously disagreed. One company commented that they had had little success with biographies of lesser-known figures; this is doubtless true and is a somewhat depressing thought – is there really nothing to be published except another life of Mary, Queen of Scots, or Winston Churchill? However, the 20th publisher accepted it and the book has gone into a second edition, so perseverance does pay!

It is also necessary to consider exactly how relevant your subject's life is to the wider picture – or at least how relevant you can make it. There is perhaps likely to be some additional difficulty in persuading a sceptical publisher that publishing the life of Ebenezer Brown is a good idea if you have to admit that nobody else adopted his innovations in pig husbandry – although there is always a certain appeal in the account of a lonely and unsuccessful struggle. In general, however, if doing this type of biography it is important to keep firmly in mind the wider audience and to take pains to root your subject's experiences in a broader historical context. Of course this means that you have inevitably to become reasonably expert not only on your subject's life but on the entire milieu in which he or she lived and worked. To be fair, you would really have to have acquired this expertise in any event, but in the case of the 'biography as illustration of subject area' this background expertise needs to be much more prominent and the two aspects – life-story and life/work environment – need to be kept in a very careful balance. Even before you start serious work on your biography, you might have a certain degree of fascination in the minutiae of your subject's life; and as you work on the project you will almost certainly succumb to such a fascination. But will your reader really want to know all this, or is there a danger of the minutiae, however interesting, swamping the bigger picture?

Understanding localities

Biographies can also be written to illustrate and increase knowledge of a locality. To some extent this overlaps with the point made above, but a life of, say, a Hebridean school-teacher, a Gloucestershire farm-worker or a Huddersfield mill-worker, while hopefully of considerable intrinsic interest, is also likely to be a valuable help in understanding that particular locality, its society and the unique features that characterise it. Here too there is a great need for the biographer to see the bigger picture, and to take pains to relate the life-experience of their subject to the generalities of life in the Hebrides or Huddersfield. They must draw out the specifics, point out the distinctive features, seek parallels with other communities and address such basic topics as change through time. How, for example, was the life of the Huddersfield mill-worker different from that of her mill-worker mother or her mill-worker daughter? Such issues as the extent to which the subject of the biography was typical or atypical of their place and time, and the broader lessons that can be drawn from their life-experience, will help to commend your book to a wider audience.

Group biographies

While most biographies are of individuals, a significant number are of groups: perhaps a family like the Kennedys or the Rothschilds, or a cultural grouping such as the literary movement known as the Bloomsbury Group. This is a very long-established form of biographical writing, with many distinguished examples: one such is the Renaissance writer Giorgio Vasari's *Lives of the Painters, Sculptors and Architects*. This approach offers interesting opportunities to trace similarities and point up differences, and also enables the life-stories of minor group-members to be brought into the bigger picture. The 'parallel lives' approach – comparing and contrasting two figures, such as Hitler and Stalin – is a variant on this and has an equally distinguished pedigree. There are major challenges in taking on such a project, not least the difficulty of keeping the narrative thread clear when one may be moving from figure to figure, but it can be a very rewarding and interesting form of biographical writing.

Exploring family history

The huge interest in family history and genealogy is a remarkable contemporary phenomenon. It may owe much to the fact that fewer and fewer of us live in the communities we were born in. Stable relationships are increasingly difficult to find, and a sense of identity needs to be deliberately sought rather than simply acquired naturally. Whatever the reason, millions of people today are busily engaged in tracing their ancestors.

While this process is interesting enough in itself, some will wish to go a step further and find out much more about their ancestors than just the 'Vital Records' type of information about births, marriages and deaths. When this happens the family-tree enthusiast becomes the family historian, or the biographer. Unless great-great-grand uncle William happened to be very famous, or his life had a wider significance and can be tied to a broader theme, or you are exceptionally lucky or talented, then this biographical work is most probably going to be non-commercial. Very possibly it will never even be published. Nevertheless there is still a need for good technique, for efficient research methods and for sensible presentation – not only for the sake of the self-esteem of the biographer, but because at some point in the future your unpublished, non-commercial life of great-great-grand uncle William may be of real value as a contribution to some other historical or biographical project. The better your work is, and the more comprehensively documented and referenced it is, the more seriously it will be taken and the more reliance will be placed on it. Great-great-grand uncle William may at last find his rightful place in somebody's bigger picture.

Telling your own story

Just as Rifleman Harris thought it worthwhile to write down his recollections of service in Spain and Portugal (see page 32), so many others through the years have wanted to write their own story, leaving for posterity an account of their life or of a part of it. Particularly as we grow older, many of us want to attempt to draw out some meaning from our lives. Writing an autobiography addresses this need. It can also be valued for its own sake as a healing process; or because there is a desire to set the record straight; or just to leave an account of one's life behind, so that death does not come as a complete extinction and to ensure that we leave what Longfellow called 'footprints on the sands of time'. By its very nature much of this autobiographical writing is of no great interest outside the confines of family and friends (and sometimes, it has to be said, of not much interest to them either!). This is hardly surprising; my own life-story is hardly, to quote Sir Philip Sidney, 'A tale which holdeth children from play and old men from the chimney corner.' As we noted in Chapter 1, the autobiographer, the personal memoir writer, can all too easily fall prey to the vanity publisher and invest large sums of money in the production of a book that nobody wants to buy.

If you are the sort of person whose autobiography will be of widespread general interest, you are probably well aware of this – and whether you are a cabinet minister, a rock star or a lone yachtswoman you will probably find little difficulty in getting a publisher, a ghost writer if necessary, and, of course, a large advance! If on the other hand you had quite an interesting war, or some other sort of fairly remarkable life-experience along with lots of other people, then regrettably it is pretty unlikely that your memoirs will become the subject of a bidding frenzy among the international publishing conglomerates. This does not, however, invalidate the process of autobiography. You may have to accept that your recollections of the Korean War or life in a Welsh coal-mine will never be commercially published, let alone top the bestseller lists – but that is no reason to give up on the idea of writing down your recollections and doing the job to the highest possible standard. Having done it, then you should think about finding some way of ensuring that your memoirs, and your unique and irreplaceable perspective, is not lost. Think about whether the regimental museum of the unit you served with in Korea would accept a copy, or whether the local public library in that Welsh mining community will accept a copy for their collection. The answer is almost certainly that both will welcome your donation with enthusiasm and gratitude. This process ensures that when somebody comes along next year or next century to write the story of your regiment in Korea or the history of Merthyr Tydfil, your recollections will be available and will greatly enrich their work – surely a very fine form of immortality, and more effective than leaving the only copy of your typescript to pass down an increasingly uninterested family tree until somebody eventually destroys it.

A special form of autobiography, and one which deserves a

separate mention, is the diary. One need only think of Pepys or Boswell to see what a distinguished history the diary has as a form of autobiography. Admittedly neither Pepys nor Boswell planned the publication of their diaries in their own lifetime (although other compulsive diarists, such as the politician Tony Benn, certainly have). Whether written with a view to publication or not, the diary has an intimacy, a presence and a directness which can be hard to recapture in the more structured form of a continuously written narrative. As with any biography or autobiography, the thing that will win readers is the interest of the life coupled with the way in which the story is told. A dull life is still a dull life even if diligently recorded in a diary every night; an interesting life told in a dull way is dull whether told in diary form or in continuous narrative. Interesting, of course, is not necessarily the same thing as famous. Many autobiographies of unknown people have been successfully published – although they are perhaps the exception that proves the rule, and their success is usually due to the quality of the writing lifting the book out of the ordinary.

4
Finding a Subject

'Natural selection'

People sometimes ask those of us who write biographies: 'How do you choose what to write about?' My usual answer to this question – that the subjects more or less choose me – sounds phoney, but there really is a great deal of truth in that, however pretentious it may seem.

It is a commonplace piece of advice to aspiring writers that they should 'write about what they know'; but commonplace or not, this is advice that holds every bit as good in writing biography as it does for the aspiring novelist or short-story writer. Most first-time biographers will have little trouble in choosing their first subject: the majority get into writing biography because of a desire to celebrate a particular life, rather than from any general desire to write biography. In my own case, my first venture into this field came because of a local connection. I grew up in the town where my subject, Henry Bell, had lived and worked and his life and achievements had formed part of my everyday experience – for example, there was a very imposing monument to him just a hundred yards away from my home. Like the rest of my fellow-citizens I thought I knew all about Bell. What turned a general interest in the man and a vague local loyalty to his memory into the level of commitment needed to spend years researching him and writing 80,000 words about him was the discovery of inconsistencies in the published material about Bell's pioneering steamboat – coupled with the slightly puzzled realisation that nobody had bothered to write a book about him since the mid-19th century.

Having been bitten by the biographical bug, the problem more often comes in finding an appropriate subject for the second or the third book. Sometimes the second subject comes along pretty naturally – if you have written about one 19th century soldier it may seem a natural step to move on to another. Having dealt with one 16th century reformer then there is logic and economy in writing about a second one, because you can usefully apply your expertise and specialist knowledge.

Sometimes, though, more obscure links and connections can lead to the selection of a subject. These connections may be very obvious to the writer but not quite so apparent to the reader – or to a publisher. There may be some merit in explaining the reasons for your choice to publishers, to convince them that there is method in your apparent madness and that you are not simply flitting about from subject to subject but working to a logical master plan. As one example, my third book-length biography came about as a direct link to the Henry Bell book. The subject, a 19th century Highland chief, Alasdair Macdonell of Glengarry, attracted my attention because he died, in rather dramatic circumstances, as a result of an accident involving one of Henry Bell's steamboats. To me the connection is obvious – but I don't imagine that it is the first thing a reader will think of. While doing a little research about Macdonell for the Bell book I decided that he was an interesting character who was probably worth some more consideration, and marked him down for future attention.

In between these two books came my life of Lord Braxfield, which, apart from being roughly contemporary with the other two and being a Scottish subject, had no other obvious links. The Braxfield book came about because a friend and I were talking about some of his quotable, if politically incorrect, remarks; things like 'Hang a thief when he is young, and he'll no' steal when he's auld', and my friend asked if anyone had ever written a biography of Braxfield. A question to which I had, of course, no immediate answer, but one which I went off to research. I found that for some reason, although there were a number of articles written about him, he had never been the subject of a book-length treatment. From that awareness of what might be called 'the state of the market in Braxfield studies' to deciding that I could usefully and enjoyably fill that gap was not too big a jump.

Looking for a subject

When deciding on a subject, one of your first steps should be to see whether anyone else has previously written a biography on them. The existence of previous work is certainly not an argument against a new treatment, but you will naturally want to know what has been said before about your subject – and the existence of other biographies will certainly be of some relevance to your potential publisher. There are a number of ways in which you can check out the competition:

- Do a search on one of the Internet bookselling sites such as http://www.amazon.co.uk or its US counterpart http://www.amazon.com. These sites have search engines which allow you to look for keywords in a title, so the name of your subject would be an appropriate term to use. My biography of the Highland chief is called *The Last of the Chiefs* – which is quite a catchy title, I think, but admittedly not a great deal of help to somebody searching for books about a man called Macdonell. However, a search on the words in the sub-title 'Alastair Ranaldson Macdonell of Glengarry 1773–1828' will bring up details of the book. As you would expect, this type of search will only provide details of titles that are currently available, although some recently out-of-print titles and some soon-to-be-published titles will also be listed.
- For a more comprehensive sweep of past and present titles, consult one of the online catalogues of a national library, such as the British Library at http://blpc.bl.uk or the US Library of Congress at http://catalog.loc.gov. Both these catalogues allow searching by author, title and keyword, so they will work – provided, of course, that your search term is somewhere in the title or sub-title. If the author of the biography has not used the subject's name in the title or sub-title then neither of these search strategies will produce a result – so, to take an imaginary example, a biography of Henry Bell called *Steamship Pioneer: a Life of the Man who Built the Comet* will not be found by a search on 'Bell' as a keyword.
- The two methods outlined above are based on the computer's ability to search swiftly through title-page information that

has been input into a database; they provide easy ways to find what has been published, and are a good first step in your research. A more thorough approach is to use tools that have analysed the contents of books and know that *Steamship Pioneer* is about Henry Bell. These do exist, although they tend to be much more difficult to access and are often more time-consuming to use than Internet sources. They are all dependent for their effectiveness on a variety of factors – that the book in question came to the notice of the compiler, that the compiler has made the right decision about the contents and the philosophy behind the work, and so on. Such sources may differ in the degree to which they provide analytical entries which will identify individual topics and contributions to multi-subject works.

Among the more useful of these sources is the Royal Historical Society's *Bibliography of British and Irish History*, now available online at http://www.rhs.ac.uk/bibl/. You can search this by author, title, keyword, location and subject classification. Of course, if your subject does not lie within the broad sweep of British and Irish history then this useful resource will be of little assistance; there exist specialised bibliographies on every subject under the sun and these can be consulted at a major library.

- For books published in the UK since 1950 the *British National Bibliography* (*BNB*) provides a comprehensive listing with author and title indexes, and also offers a classified approach using the Dewey Decimal Classification. If you wish to see whether a biography of, say, a particular coalminer has been published then you would find the Dewey number for coal-mining and search the classified section of the *BNB* for possible entries.

- A useful guide to biographical writing is the two-volume *Biographical Books* published by R R Bowker, New York, which covers biographies published in or distributed in the United States from 1876 to 1980. This has a vocation index, so that you can see all the biographies of, for example, all botanists published between these dates; it also has a name/subject index, an author index and a title index. Despite its focus on the US this is a valuable tool for the UK researcher, as many titles published in the UK are included because they were distributed in the US.

- If you can identify a book on the same subject as yours, or on a closely related topic, this gives you a useful starting point. Check out the bibliography – the list of works consulted or referred to that usually appears at the back of most scholarly books – and see what another author has found published on the subject in which you are interested.

Sometimes, they find you

Subjects come to the notice of the biographer in a variety of ways, and the more you write in the biographical field the more potential subjects will attract your attention. Sometimes something that you read will suggest a subject – a passing reference, an intriguing quote, a general sense that there is an interesting character out there waiting to be explored. Sometimes the idea for a biography can be sparked off by something quite non-literary: an artefact, a building, a monument. I wrote an article about George Buchanan, a 16th century Scottish scholar and reformer, simply because I was struck by the size of the monument to him which had been erected at Killearn in Stirlingshire. The monument, an obelisk 103 feet high, towers over the little village. My reaction to it was that it was exactly the sort of thing that might be expected to mark the site of a great battle or the birthplace of a national hero, not the birthplace of a rather obscure scholar. Buchanan's life, which I would certainly not feel competent to deal with at length, sold as a 2500-word article and demonstrates that one can deal with a subject adequately, at a certain level, even if one lacks the skills and background to do a more comprehensive and original piece of work. Buchanan, for example, wrote mostly in Latin and lived for a long time in France – so it would be very difficult to write an original and serious extended biography of him without considerable skills in Latin and French. However, for the purposes of an article designed for a popular magazine, secondary sources and the ability to put the subject into context and to interpret other people's research for a general audience are often all that is required.

Subjects come up in other ways too. Sometimes friends and

relatives, knowing the sort of thing that you write, will suggest subjects to you. Once book and magazine publishers are aware of your skills or interests, they will sometimes suggest subjects that they would like to see covered. This is very encouraging and enormously good for one's self-esteem, and there is a huge advantage in having a commission and not having to worry about cold-selling the finished work to a publisher. However, the prospect of a secure commission should not blind you to the other considerations that need to be taken into account when selecting a subject:

- Have you the skills to do justice to the topic? Do you need to be able to read Latin, decipher 15th century handwriting or understand nuclear fission?
- Does the subject interest you? A biography takes a long time to write; if the subject bores you it will seem to take a great deal longer and your lack of enjoyment may become all too apparent in your writing.
- Would you rather be doing something else? Even if the subject seems interesting you might feel that your priorities lie elsewhere.
- How will this project fit into the overall pattern of your writing career? If you feel that you want to specialise in writing the lives of members of the women's suffrage movement, would taking a year or two out to write the life of a Boer War general be a good idea?
- Can you cope with the subject in practical terms? Are the papers you would need to use in an archive in Aberdeen while you live in Bristol? Are there essential official documents that you will not be able to access for your research because they are unavailable until a certain date?

All of these points are things that you should take into consideration in choosing any subject, but they perhaps need a second or a third thought before you are seduced by the prospect of a commission. It is all too easy to go along with an idea when it is pitched to you by a publisher or editor, and then to find out, when you are launched on the project, that it involves significant problems. If you have evolved your project yourself, you are more likely to have had a chance to feel your way into the subject and into its associated challenges and opportunities.

Basic planning and preparation

However the idea for your biography comes about, before you commit yourself to any work on it you need to do some serious thinking, planning and preparation. Some of the issues that need to be determined at this planning stage include:

- *The extent of the work.* Is this a magazine article or a book? A long book or a short book? How long are you going to have to commit to the project to do it successfully, and is this economically viable?
- *The scope of the work.* Are you going to write about the entire life of your subject, or just one chronological period – or just one aspect of it?
- *The level of the work.* Is this for a general or a specialist audience, for adults or teenagers or children?
- *The skills you need to acquire to do justice to the subject.* Do you need to learn how to read early handwriting, become familiar with the organisation of the Royal Navy in the 18th century, or know the working of an early 20th century repertory theatre?
- *Your sources.* Are the sources that you can conveniently access sufficient for the work you are planning? While for a popular magazine article you can usually safely rely on secondary sources, a more scholarly book will require the use of original materials; these may simply not be available, or may be available but located somewhere inconvenient. There is nothing more annoying than spending valuable time on a project only to find, part-way through, that there are simply not the sources available to you to allow you to do justice to it.
- *Financial considerations.* How are you going to finance the project? What will the costs be? Think of things like photocopying, travel and subsistence, the acquisition of illustrations. Is there an advance from your publisher? What are you going to live on while you are writing the book?
- *Further opportunities.* What opportunities are there for a multiple exploitation of the project? If you are writing a full-

length biography, can you promote the book and earn some additional fees by writing articles based on it, developing radio or television spin-offs, or lecturing about it? Are there 'detachable' parts of the project which can be developed? This may be something that you will only discover as you go along – but it is well worth keeping in mind throughout the entire process. There may very well be an aspect of your subject's life that merits treatment at greater length than you can afford within the confines of your book or article. There may be a subsidiary character who comes into your biography but cannot be properly dealt with there. Such subsidiary themes can be usefully developed and marketed as stand-alone articles and often require very little extra work to complete. All these additional ways of exploiting your subject may make the difference between an economically unviable project and one that may be worth pursuing.

This said, I must admit that none of my three biographies has, as yet, been economically viable if all the costs – of time, travel, research expenses such as photocopying, stationery, book purchases and so on – are costed in. Despite this, I do not regret having taken any of them on!

5

Thinking About Structure

Be flexible!

To a very considerable extent, the emerging story of the life that you are writing, and the research that you will do while writing it, will determine how you structure your biography or autobiography. If you approach biographical writing with a cast-iron concept about structure, then the constraints that this will put on your research and writing are likely to lead you into some very real difficulties. There is always a need to be able to change and adapt your concepts as the pattern of the life unfolds. You also need to be intellectually open and honest enough to follow the trail that the evidence presents to you, even if it is going to take you in unexpected directions – directions that may at times be quite unwelcome and unsettling.

You may find unexpected information about your subject which will totally alter your preconceived notions about them, and you need to be able to respond appropriately to such new information. For example you may, in the course of your research, discover for the first time that your subject had been a conscientious objector in the First World War or had contracted a bigamous marriage or had written a novel under an assumed name. Such information must be allowed to shape your work, and may require a major re-casting of your planned structure. You may also find, in the course of your research and writing, that it is simply not possible to complete the book you had planned. Perhaps you hit a major obstacle by way of an unanticipated lack of sources, or perhaps you are denied access to the sources that you need to do a good job. You may even find, as has happened to me, that somebody else is working on a similar project so that an essential private archive is closed to other researchers at present, or that somebody else is so far advanced

46

in writing about the same subject that you feel it pointless to attempt to compete.

How you react to these circumstances will depend on the scale of the problem, but they are all likely to require a substantial change of plans. Will changing the focus of your book get around the problem or can a shortage of sources in one area be compensated for in another? Almost certainly, the least satisfactory response is to stick doggedly to your original plan; far better to think again and adapt to the changed circumstances – trying some other form of publication, for example, such as a series of articles rather than a book. At worst you may just feel that you have to cut your losses and move on to another subject.

Finding a focus

Although you need to remain flexible and move where the sources lead you, the old military adage about 'time spent in reconnaissance never being wasted' holds good for biographers too. Before investing too much time and energy in a project, plan in some detail what you are going to do, whether you can achieve it, and how it might be structured. Giving some serious preliminary thought to structure is vital and this process can be conveniently combined with the planning and scoping exercise outlined at the end of Chapter 4. Thinking about structure is extremely helpful in determining what sort of research you are going to have to undertake and where the possible difficulties in your research may arise. If, for example, your subject spent 15 significant years of his life diamond-mining in South Africa, then knowing that you have to cover such a large part of his life will force you to think about how you can research this, what the sources for that period will be, and even whether you can give a coherent account of it without seeing a diamond mine or visiting South Africa.

The first key point to determine is whether your book is going to cover the subject's entire life or only deal with a part of it. If the really interesting part of the life that you are going to write about is four years spent as a missionary in China, or six years spent as a bomber pilot or nine years spent as a Member of Parliament, then do you really need to write about the other 70 years in detail? Would a brief preliminary section setting the interesting bit in context, and a brief concluding section telling what happened after your subject stopped being a missionary (or bomber pilot, or MP), not be enough for most readers? Few subjects have had a totally enthralling life from birth to death; and you are not obliged to provide a detailed account of an unremarkable childhood and a dull but respectable career in banking that 'topped and tailed' six exciting years as a bomber pilot.

Biographers naturally get fascinated by their subjects, but they also need to remember that their audience may not totally share that fascination. The potential reader is basically looking for a good read and may well wonder why all this extraneous information is being given. Of course, if there are important childhood experiences which shaped the adult in a very significant way – your Member of Parliament met Lloyd George as a little boy, or your missionary had a conversion experience at the age of 11 – then you will definitely need to include this, but otherwise have some pity for your potential readers and spare them a detailed account of the humdrum and unremarkable.

Indeed, it is a good general rule that the writer needs to select the significant and the revealing rather than just pile up fact upon fact. It is a frequent and fair criticism of many biographies that they are far too long and far too detailed, and that the interesting and relevant parts get swamped by the repetitive and mundane ones. Some biographies appear to be not so much texts to be read for enjoyment and instruction as quarries from which facts and other texts can be extracted.

It may well be that once you decide to focus on your subject's years as a missionary in China, this will not provide enough material for a book. Remember there is no rule which says that every biography has to be 500 pages long, and there are some splendid examples of quite short texts which have achieved both critical and commercial success – Dava Sobel's *Longitude* is one case in point. If your story does not look like providing enough material for a book then perhaps you should consider magazine publication. Alternatively you could explore the possibilities of a group biography – the lives of three or four missionaries, for example.

If you decide to write about a whole life, then do not feel embarrassed about skipping over periods when nothing very important happens. Obviously you need to be sure that nothing important actually *did* happen, and that the apparent lack of incident is not simply a reflection of inadequate sources; but if the sources are inadequate for a period then there is no harm in admitting it – 'We do not know what Mary Brown did between the ages of 23 and 28.' – This is certainly better than ignoring the 'missing' years, attempting to conceal your lack of information or padding that section out with uninteresting material.

A strong opening

You also need to give some thought to how your subject's life might best be laid out for the reader. The most obvious starting point is their birth: 'John Brown was born on 23rd April 1889 in the back bedroom at 234 High Street, Bradford.' However, the most obvious way is not always the best way. I find something slightly depressing about a biography that starts, 'John Brown was born…', because I have a strong feeling that on the last page I will come to a description of John Brown's funeral. The fact that you are writing the story of a life does not mean that you have to slavishly follow it from beginning to end. There may be a strong argument in favour of finding a different, and perhaps more commercially focused and attractive, structure – particularly if your biography is about a lesser-known character. Quite properly, in your planning and writing there needs to be an element of 'selling the subject': your theme needs to be sold, first of all to the publisher who has to buy the piece, and secondly to the readers who have to commit their time to reading it and perhaps their money to buying it. If the subject of your book is not a household name then simply starting off with their birth is not likely to provide the most enticing introduction.

There is much truth in the old cliché about only having one chance to make a good first impression. The publisher or the reader might reasonably ask why they should bother to publish or read this particular book, so your first chapter could often be better devoted to recounting an interesting and significant incident from the subject's life, or to a brief explanation of the subject's claim to fame or place in history, rather than to the chronologically appropriate discussion of family background or early years at school. It is all a matter of making connections – trying to find a point of reference for the reader or creating a way for them to feel attuned to the subject of the biography. This is not to suggest that family background and early years at school may not be important elements – just that they need not be the first thing you present.

My biography of Henry Bell was structured in just this sort of way. I felt that a description of the first voyage of his pioneering steamship *Comet*, its significance and its consequences, provided the strongest opening for the book. It would go some way to explaining who this man Bell was, and what he had done that was worthy of note more than a century and a half after his death; with any luck, it would also would encourage the reader to make a commitment to reading the rest of the book. Once the reader has gone the length of reading your first chapter and is 'on board' then you can safely feed in the interesting and useful, but perhaps not extremely exciting, information about your subject's parents, and where he or she was born, grew up and was educated.

Chronology – and the alternatives

Nor does the rest of the book need to follow a rigid chronological sequence. Although this is usually easier to write, and possibly easier for the reader to understand, there may be very strong reasons to break away at times from an adherence to strict chronology. For example, there may be themes in your subject's life that recur. If you want to discuss, say, his three marriages, it might make sense to deal with one, two or all of these outside the normal chronological time sequence – at least the possibility of doing so should be seriously considered. It is sometimes rewarding to interweave such topic-driven sections or chapters through what is basically a straightforward chronological structure, as it allows the author and reader to explore related topics which may be widely distant in time and can also provide a welcome change of pace from the narrative drive. So, choosing the best possible structure for a book is one of the biographer's key tasks, and one which should not be neglected or taken lightly. There is always a choice, and even if you think that the choice you have made is correct, you should have worked through at least some of the other options and be clear about why you feel them to be less desirable. You will feel much happier writing the book if you know that the structure you are creating has been carefully planned and the book is not just a loosely connected assemblage of facts.

Even if you settle on a straightforward chronological narrative there is still the question of how to arrange the internal divisions within that narrative. Real lives tend to be governed by forces other than calendars and clocks, so dividing your narrative by decades or years is not usually going to provide the most satisfactory solution to internal structure. Better, in most cases, to look for significant turning-points in your subject's career and let these determine your sub-divisions. Of course, this will tend to make for uneven chapter lengths – but this is a very small price to pay for a robust structure that presents your subject's life in a clear and accessible way.

It can be very useful at this stage to think of a title for each chapter. These may well change as the work advances, but the exercise will keep your mind on what you are actually writing and force a desirable concentration on the main themes of your narrative. If, for example, your character spends a year travelling around Europe, you may deal with this in a chapter called 'The Grand Tour'. During this time, back home, his father re-marries; do you include the story of this re-marriage in 'The Grand Tour' or should it form part of another chapter? Obviously there are no hard-and-fast rules about this sort of thing, but having chapter titles at an early stage will help you to focus on structural and presentational issues in a way that 'Chapter 7' won't. Such chapter titles are also very helpful when preparing a synopsis and selling an idea to a publisher. At a later stage your definitive chapter titles provide the reader with a helpful navigational device, giving them a clue as to where you are taking them and what they might expect from this stage in the journey.

When you get to the stage of identifying chapters and chapter titles, you should also note down what the broad content of each chapter might be. During the writing process you can then refer to your outline and see whether all aspects of the life have been covered – and if so, whether they have been covered in the right amount of detail and in the best order. It is never too late for change, of course, but there is a great deal of sense in plotting out, as early as possible, the most attractive, understandable and convenient way of presenting your information. Again, this is a good time to think about what is significant and what is not. Some 'insignificant' material will certainly find its way in – and it may be very well worth keeping if it provides colour and background; but an outline plan will help you to keep control over your work and sharpen your sense of priorities.

Balance and context

Another issue you could consider at this planning stage is the balance between your subject's personal life and their career or public life. While much of the decision-making on this will come as you actually write the text, (see Chapter 8), it does merit some thought, in broad outline at least, early on. Some subjects will lead a 'divided' life with little obvious cross-over from the personal into the public, while others – and perhaps this is particularly true of artists and writers – are enormously influenced in their work by their personal lives and relationships. In your biographical project the two elements will therefore need to be dealt with in an integrated way.

In Chapter 1, we looked at the problem of providing background information to help your reader understand the context of your story. In thinking about the possible structure of your biography this question has to be kept in mind, and some strategic decisions taken about the way that this contextual information is to be delivered on the page as part of your narrative. It is important to remember that you are writing a biography and not a history, so the main character must not be allowed to disappear for too long while you set the scene, discuss finer points of historical interpretation or outline the shortcomings of previous biographers.

Illustrations

Although it might not seem much to do with structure, it can be very useful – even at this early stage – to give some thought to the pictures that you may eventually use as illustrations for your biography. (And if you believe the old saying about 'one picture being worth a thousand words', then perhaps the question of illustrations is, quite genuinely, a structural one.)

What sort of illustrations you will use and how many you will need are matters that are likely to be discussed in detail when the biography is completed and has found a publisher. However, the matter should always be at the back of your mind. As you do your research for the book you will undoubtedly come across potential illustrations, and if you are always on the alert for them then they will tend to be more easily spotted. It is far simpler to note down the details at the time, and to establish costs and procedures for obtaining copies, than have to search for them again months or years later.

What to call it – titles as a selling-point

If chapter titles are important, then the overall title for your book (or article) is vital. The right title will go a long way to selling your book; the wrong one will not only limit your sales but can cause real problems by raising false expectations in the reader's mind.

Your publisher will probably have very firm ideas about the title, even if they can sometimes seem not to have too many other firm ideas about your book. A good title can be elusive but is worth searching for because it has a lot of work to do. It should be sufficiently interesting to attract the reader's attention, so *My Life* is probably not a good choice; it should be understandable, so an obscure quotation or literary reference may not work well; it should be sufficiently brief to be memorable, capable of being assimilated in a glance and capable of being translated into an eye-catching cover design. It should also, preferably, be unique, so as to avoid confusion with other books.

To deal with the last problem first: there is no copyright in book titles, so there is no legal reason why your memoirs cannot be called *War and Peace* or your next biography be published as *Pride and Prejudice*. There is however the possibility of titles being protected as trademarks, or of action being taken if you attempt to pass off your work as something else – so even if your name is H Potter and you are a lecturer in philosophy, I would think twice before calling your memoirs *Harry Potter and the Philosopher's Stone*. In practice there are always likely to be books on the market with the same title as your preferred one, and it would be very hard to say that you should not use it – particularly if, as is often the case, the other book deals with a very different subject. There are also areas where use of the same title is probably inevitable: textbooks, for example, with titles like *Basic Economics* or *Elementary Algebra* which are more frequently distinguished by their author's name.

As we discussed in Chapter 4, computerised catalogues and other 'finding tools' make it desirable that your subject's name should appear somewhere on the title page – either in the title or in the sub-title – as this has a huge impact on the ability of an enquirer to trace your book. It then becomes, to some extent, a matter of taste whether the subject's name forms the title with a descriptive, intriguing or distinguishing sub-title – as in Claire Tomalin's award-winning *Samuel Pepys: the Unequalled Self* – or whether the reverse procedure is adopted, as in Mark Urban's *The Man who Broke Napoleon's Codes: the Story of George Scovell*. These two examples probably do suggest a useful rule. If your subject is very well known, like Pepys, then their name will help to sell the book and could usefully come first. If on the other hand your subject is hardly a household name (like George Scovell), then commercial prudence suggests that you should find a title that conveys something of what the person's claim to fame is – or at least something that is sufficiently intriguing to make the browser pick the book up or click on the 'more information' button on the bookshop's web page.

The ideal title is short, distinctive, memorable, easily pronounced and unembarrassing to ask for in a bookshop or library. Try to avoid being too clever, and try not to become too attached to your title – because there is a fair chance that somebody will decide it needs to be changed. One book of mine got through all the stages of writing and production right up to its presentation at the publisher's sales meeting, at which point the sales force argued forcefully (and in retrospect probably correctly) that they could not go out on the road and sell a book with that title! I write quite often for an American magazine and find that they change my article titles in about 50% of cases – usually in my view for the worse, but while they continue to buy the articles I just grin and bear their choices. Even when you have done a lot of careful research into your title there may be a very compelling, but not immediately obvious, reason for a publisher to change it – for example, they may have another book in production with a title that is confusingly similar to yours.

The search for the right title can be a long one – and sometimes the right title is amazingly hard to find. This is certainly an area where the more bright ideas you can pull together, the better; and it is an area where you can usefully canvass opinions from friends and family. A good title can really boost sales, but unfortunately there are no rules to follow. A classic case in point is one of the non-fiction bestsellers of the 1950s. When its publisher announced the forthcoming book, he was told by the majority of the trade that a book with an unintelligible title, by a foreign author with an unpronounceable name, would never succeed. However, Thor Heyerdahl's *Kon-tiki Expedition* sold vast quantities, is still selling, and the publisher laughed all the way to the bank. Whether or not this is the exception that proves the rule, there is little doubt that a title that is instantly accessible, and which a buyer or borrower can ask for without feeling foolish, is a great advantage – so perhaps *Peter Piper's Peck of Pickled Peppers* is not the best possible title for your memoirs, and the days when a title like *Biographia Literaria* flew off the bookshop shelves are probably gone.

6

Starting Your Research

The question of how to go about your research can be a remarkably difficult one to answer. As we discussed in Chapter 1, for each individual you write about, your sources of information will be quite different. For some subjects you will have abundant, even apparently excessive, sources; while for others there will be a definite dearth of information. For this reason, any advice given in this chapter cannot be comprehensive: it can only point you in potentially useful directions.

The basic printed sources

As with any research, the first place to start is with the obvious and traditional sources, and to ensure that you take full advantage of all the work that has already been done. This means looking at the range of standard printed reference sources, most of which can be found in large libraries. (See Chapter 12 for a list of the major research libraries.) We are fortunate to have available for our use as biographers a huge range of printed sources – sources which can, more often than one might think, give a starting point for research and a basic framework to the life-story of our subjects. There is perhaps a tendency to think that these printed sources only deal with the 'great and the good' and that 'ordinary' people are not included. In fact, the range of people covered tends to be a great deal wider than might at first be assumed.

One of the key works that should certainly be consulted is *The Dictionary of National Biography*, published by Oxford University Press. Originally a product of the Victorian age, this work – familiarly known as the *DNB* – has been continually augmented over the years and the original volumes now have many supplementary volumes. A completely new edition, to be known as the *Oxford Dictionary of National Biography*, is in preparation and is due for publication in print and electronic formats in September 2004. A deliberate effort has been made to widen the scope of the work and to ensure that certain categories of people who were previously seriously under-represented are now covered. The electronic version of the *Oxford Dictionary of National Biography* will provide powerful search facilities: for example, it will enable a search to be made for all people born in, say, Doncaster, or all subjects who died in 1823, or all those biographees who were botanists. The 60 volumes of the print edition will cost £7500 and so it is unlikely to appear on the shelves of your village branch library, but it should be available in central libraries and at major reference service points.

Despite its more limited social and occupational scope, the original *DNB* includes a surprising number of people from outside what might be seen as the traditional social and political elites. Even if you are fairly certain that your subject was far too low in status ever to be included in the *DNB*, you should check. It is also worth checking entries for their parents, children or spouses – a close relative may have qualified for an entry and their entry may include significant information about other family members.

There are now a large number of similar National Biography projects in other countries and these may be of use to you if your subject came to the United Kingdom from abroad, or emigrated. One example is the *American National Biography* (edited by J A Garratty & M C Carnes, New York, Oxford UP, 1999).

There are also general biographical dictionaries which can readily be consulted – works such as *Chambers Biographical Dictionary* (7th edition edited by Una McGovern, Edinburgh, Chambers, 2002) and *Who's Who* (London, A & C Black), which has been published annually since 1849 and which aims to provide information on 'people who through their careers affect the political, economic, scientific and artistic life of the country'. Then there are the specialist biographical sources such as *Who's Who of British Members of Parliament* 1832–1979 (4 volumes, edited by Michael Stenton & Stephen Lees, Hassocks,

Harvester Press, 1976–1981) or *Commissioned Sea-officers of the Royal Navy 1660–1815* (D Syrett & R L DiNardo, Aldershot, Scolar Press, 1994) and ambitious large-scale biographical sources such as Emmanuel Bénézit's ten-volume *Dictionnaire critique et documentaire des peintres, sculpteurs, dessinateurs et graveurs de tous temps et de tous les pays ...* Paris, Gründ, c1976. Indeed, most occupational groups you can think of, such as writers, engineers, philosophers and botanists, have their own dedicated biographical sources, and you can trace these works through a major library.

Generally speaking the *DNB*-type of publication requires its subjects to be dead before they are included, while the *Who's Who* type of publication deals with living figures. Works like *Who's Who* may be particularly useful if you can access back-runs of them and thereby obtain information on people who had perhaps a temporary significance in some field or other but are less likely to find their way into the universal biographical sources. The publishers of *Who's Who* very usefully transfer the entries for dead *Who's Who* subjects into periodic cumulations called *Who Was Who*, of which there have so far been nine volumes covering the period from 1895 to 1995 and an overall index volume.

Inevitably, although such printed reference sources are increasingly widening their scope, most still concentrate on the social, economic and political elites – who in consequence tend to be a very well-documented group. For the upper social classes there is a wide range of reference sources, such as *Debrett's Peerage and Baronetage* (London, Debrett, 2000) which has been published since 1769; *Burke's Peerage and Baronetage* (Granz [Switzerland], Burke's Peerage, 1999) now in its 106th edition; and *Burke's Genealogical and Heraldic History of the Landed Gentry* (London, Burke's Peerage, 1972), now in its 18th edition. None of these will be of much use to you in tracing the life-story of a Dorset farm labourer – but might provide useful information on the life of the farm labourer's landlord.

Prior to the 20th century, to occupy an official position and to have undertaken higher education were two fairly sure ways of getting into printed reference works. We have already mentioned the *Who's Who of British Members of Parliament* – but further information on politicians can be found in works like

Dod's Parliamentary Companion (London, Vacher Dod Publishing) which has been providing biographical information on members of both Houses of Parliament since 1832. Officers in the British armed forces appear in the *Army List*, *Navy List* and *Air Force List* – now published by the Ministry of Defence but continuing a series of lists stretching back to 1714 in the case of the army, and to 1782 in that of the navy.

Churches have always been efficient at recording the lives and careers of the clergy – the Anglican clergy being covered by *Crockford's Clerical Directory* (London, Oxford University Press) which has been published more or less annually since 1858. The clergy of the Church of Scotland are splendidly documented in *Fasti Ecclesiae Scoticanae – the Succession of the Ministers in the Church of Scotland* (Edinburgh, Clark, dates various) which in 11 volumes records the ministers of every parish church in Scotland since the Reformation. Other denominations have produced similar historical surveys and most denominations produce a yearbook giving details of clergy and churches.

Perhaps predictably, lawyers too have managed to document themselves very thoroughly. Works like *The Inns of Court Calendar, a Record of the Members of the English Bar ...* (London, 1877) or *The Faculty of Advocates in Scotland, 1532–1943, edited by Francis J Grant* (Edinburgh, Scottish Record Society, 1944) are among the type of publications which you might consult if your subject was a lawyer.

Newspapers and periodicals provide a wealth of biographical information, although there are serious difficulties in accessing it due to a lack of indexing for many titles (and to poor and inconsistent indexing where it does exist). However, as will be discussed on pp. 77–8 under *Online sources*, this situation is improving.

Of British newspaper titles, the longest indexed run is *The Times* – for which a printed index, *Palmer's Index to* The Times *newspaper*, is available from 1790. Unfortunately *Palmer's Index* is hard to use, with oddly idiosyncratic index terms being chosen such as 'Unfortunate occurrence at Bournemouth' or 'Sad death at Hackney' that are not immediately helpful. Indexes do exist for other regional and local newspapers and the reference department of a public library in your area of interest should be able to advise you on what has been done and how such indexes can be accessed.

Some of the long-established periodicals provide valuable biographical information. Works like *The Gentleman's Magazine and Historical Chronicle* (1736–1922) or *The Scots Magazine* (1739 to date) in their 18th and 19th century issues provide some notices of births, marriages and deaths together with notices of official appointments and military promotions. These can be a very significant source of information, particularly in respect of their obituary articles. Many of the serious broadsheet newspapers have long made a feature of their obituary coverage, and collections such as *Obituaries from* The Times (London, Newspaper Archive Developments, dates various) provide a useful tool for the biographer. The obituaries were frequently written by friends or close associates of the deceased and can give intimate glimpses of their life and personality – even if at times the language used needs a degree of decoding. 'X did not suffer fools gladly' probably means that X was unbearably bad-tempered!

For background reading and general information you will need to consult non-biographical sources. Guides to reference works can direct you to the relevant resources for your area of interest – perhaps the most useful of these is *Walford's Guide to Reference Material.* * A similar work from an American background is Balay, Robert: *Guide to Reference Books* 11th ed. Chicago, American Library Association, 1996. The bibliographies attached to articles in major encyclopaedias such as *Britannica* or *Colliers* are also good sources to point you towards standard printed resources.

Local archives and libraries

All these printed sources are worth checking. However, even if your subject is well covered by them, to write a full biography

* *Vol. 1 Science & Technology*, edited by M Mullay & P Schlicke, 7th ed. London, Library Association Publishing, 1996; *Vol. 2 Social & Historical Sciences, Philosophy & Religion*, edited by A Day & M Walsh, 7th ed. London, Library Association Publishing, 1998; *Vol. 3 Generalia, Language & Literature, The Arts*, edited by A Chalcraft *et al*, 5th ed. London, Library Association Publishing, 1991

you will still need to go beyond what has been recorded in reference books and find primary source material. There is no doubt that this is the most difficult area of research because there are no hard-and-fast rules about where to look for things. Archive items turn up in the most improbable places and in collections where one would not logically expect to find them.

Local public libraries and archives obviously attempt to collect all material relevant to their areas but they also, by a variety of routes, acquire material which might seem to have no very obvious local connection. While researching my book on Henry Bell I found two very important letters by him in the collection of a library with no obvious geographical or other connection with Bell, or with the recipient of the letters. I would never have thought to seek such letters there, but found out subsequently that, in the 19th century, a local resident had been a keen collector of historical autographs and had purchased these two letters by Bell for his collection. On his death the collection he had created passed to the local library – perfectly logical if you know the story, but baffling otherwise.

There are of course ways to trace such archive collections – through the National Register of Archives for example, which exists to help you do just that and publishes, in print and electronic formats, guides to the contents of archive collections. These are widely available at major libraries and archives.

Across the United Kingdom, the biographer can find a huge range of resources at public libraries and local archive offices. All public library services have some form of local studies department, usually located in their central library; in the vast majority of cases the local studies service is well developed and considered by the library service as a priority area – as it should be, because it is the one field in which each local library has a unique opportunity to achieve excellence, and a clear remit to collect, preserve and make available the literature and records of their area.

The range of specific resources that might be found in a local studies library or archive is so huge that it is probably pointless to attempt to list them all. The following are some typical forms of material that might be generally available, and some suggestions as to how they might be applied to your biographical research:

- Voters Rolls or Registers of Electors
  + Provide evidence for residence and some indication of socio-economic status.
  + Increasingly valuable as the franchise was extended in the late 19th and 20th centuries – in the earlier period will not include women. As women got the vote in municipal elections (1869 for single women) and later in parliamentary elections (1918 for women over 30 and 1928 for women over 21) the scope and usefulness of these rolls becomes greater.
- Valuation Rolls
  + Useful for establishing property ownership and an indicator (by the valuation of the property) of socio-economic status – at times gives occupational information.
  + Frequently available from mid-19th century onwards.
  + There may be much earlier forms of local tax records such as Hearth Tax or Window Tax.
- School Records
  + Admission registers and school log books have often been preserved and can provide both specific information on your subject and background information on this aspect of local life. Many school log books are very revealing social documents reflecting interesting aspects of life outside the classroom – for example, the impact of epidemic disease (children dying of cholera or being removed due to tuberculosis), or the cycle of the agricultural year (children being kept away from school to help bring in the harvest).
- Welfare Records
  + Among the many types of social welfare records that may be preserved locally and may be relevant to your research are admission registers for poorhouses or workhouses (paupers admitted to institutional care), records of payment of 'outdoor relief' – payments in cash or kind to paupers still able to remain at home.
  + Medical records associated with poorhouses sometimes survive and can be informative.
- Local Authority Records
  + These could include the minute books of the local authority and its predecessors, as well as documents relating to a wide range of topics that came under a local council's charge: local planning and building control, health, welfare,

education, markets, streets and pavements, etc.

+ Particularly valuable for biographical purposes may be the records of local burial grounds – churchyards and local authority cemeteries.

+ Local authorities maintained burgess rolls – rolls of those citizens eligible to trade, vote and be elected to the council. These are extremely important documents for earlier periods with a very restricted franchise and when other sources are severely limited they can give valuable information, for example on the parents of the burgess. A typical form of entry might be 'John Smith, weaver, admitted burgess 1st February 1750 by right of his father William Smith, merchant, deceased'.

• Church Records

+ Many local archives hold church records, and these can include such basic genealogical information as birth, marriage and death records.

+ Church records are also of potential value in a far wider context. There may be references to employment – not just of clergy, but also of schoolteachers and the personnel responsible for the care and maintenance of church property. The building, repair and maintenance of churches and other church properties (vicarages, manses, schools, halls, etc.) may also be documented in such records.

+ Churches were also involved in a wide range of social measure and welfare provision – the distribution of money to the poor, for example. They were also involved with matters of sexual morality and social conduct and you may find references to your subject appearing before a church court as an unmarried mother, a fornicator, or a Sabbath-breaker.

• Gifts and Deposits

+ Many of the above groups of records were official or semi-official archives which would naturally find their way to a local authority archive office or library. These institutions have also, over the years, collected a far wider range of material and have actively encouraged the deposition of archival material from individuals and corporate bodies. Often these are categorised as Gifts and Deposits and frequently prove to be the richest and most valuable archives in such centres.

They might include:

- *Estate records.* The papers created by a local landed estate and deposited with the archive could include such items as wage-books, correspondence, photographs and other visual materials, estate plans and architectural drawings, contracts, leases, rental agreements, legal documents. While such records could be of great value to the biographer of a member of the estate-owning family, they can also be immensely valuable to the biographer of an estate employee. Not only is there a very reasonable chance of finding a direct reference to your subject in such papers, but the whole context of his or her life will be displayed in the evidence to be gleaned from such records.

- *Business records.* Many industrial and commercial concerns have deposited older records with local archives. Alternatively, their business archives may have been saved when the company closed, merged or moved. The range of information which can be gleaned from such collections can be huge: sources might range from formal accounting and legal records, through wage-books and correspondence, down to such things as samples of advertising material and illustrations of industrial processes. A particularly valuable sub-group of business records is the archive of business papers created by a local firm of solicitors. Many lawyers were very significant local figures and played leading roles in local political, charitable, social, and religious bodies. The records of these local institutions are often found to be inextricably mixed with the lawyer's business papers.

- *Archives of local institutions.* These can range from records of local trade incorporations, craft guilds and charitable bodies to the archives of the local tennis club or horticultural society.

- Local Newspapers
  - These may have been indexed in whole or in part by the local library and can constitute a particularly valuable source of information. Your subject may appear in a wide variety of roles – in news reports, as a letter writer, listed as a prize-winner at local events and finally, perhaps, as the

subject of an informative obituary or at least a notice in the Deaths column.

+ Bear in mind that local newspapers are not necessarily accurate or unbiased – now or in the past – and there is a need for healthy scepticism when reading their reports. There is a strong temptation to believe what is printed, especially in old newspapers, but all too often the paper got things wrong or wrote the story in a way that made perfect sense at the time but is now hard to interpret. Remember too that the local (or the national) newspaper article was not created as a reference tool or a source for your biography – it was often written with incomplete information, perhaps to conform to the political prejudices of the journalist, the editor, proprietor or readers, and would frequently be composed to a deadline with the compositor anxiously waiting for copy.

• Local Directories
  + Sometimes known as Post Office Directories. These are seldom comprehensive – the poorest residents usually do not feature in them – but given their limitations, where they exist they are key sources. They are most commonly found in major towns and cities and are less commonly available for rural areas. It can be difficult to work out who is included in them and the precise date on which they were made up.
  + They usually consist of an alphabetical listing of property-owners and tenants and often also a street-by-street listing. Very often they give occupations for the householder.
  + In addition to the residential information they frequently give comprehensive information on justices of the peace and magistrates, local government, local societies, charities and institutions, and the volunteer movement – indeed, on the whole fabric of local society.

Among the many additional resources that you might find in a typical local studies library or archive is the whole range of locally published books, pamphlets and periodicals. Many of these will be of interest to the biographer either as direct sources of information about a subject or for background information on their period and environment. Often, the older local histories are extremely detailed and, if not always enthralling reading, do provide a great deal of raw material for the biographer.

Many such centres hold transcriptions of old gravestones which can be significant sources for the period before compulsory state registration of death (1837 in England and Wales, 1855 in Scotland, 1864 in Ireland). These transcriptions are particularly important because in the years since the transcriptions were made, many gravestones have become increasingly illegible or have been removed. Photographs, prints, drawings and paintings are also actively collected and many libraries run, or have run, programmes to photographically record significant local events, townscape changes, buildings, industries, etc. These pictorial collections can be of considerable help to the biographer in getting a feel for an area's past – and of course as a fruitful source of illustrations for your book or article.

Perhaps the greatest resource that a local studies library or local archive has is its librarians or archivists. Such staff members are usually extremely well versed in the history of their areas and even more expert in the literature and documents relating to it. They can usually suggest profitable lines of research and save you a great deal of wasted time and effort by steering you away from unrewarding sources. While they cannot do your research for you, they can help, advise, and facilitate it and will often go beyond what you might reasonably expect in the provision of assistance. Talking to such staff about your research and the direction of your work is time well spent: working daily with the collection, they will frequently know exactly where to find the information you need and be able to suggest sources that you would never have thought to check. If you want to discuss your research in any detail it might be worth finding out the best time to visit. Library staffing can vary from day to day, and you are likely to get better attention if you can call when a professional librarian or archivist, rather than a library assistant, is on duty and at a time when he or she is not under pressure from other visitors.

Apart from local-authority-run libraries and archives, there are a great many other local archives throughout the country whose resources can be of critical importance to the researcher. The institutions mentioned above are all fairly clearly established to provide some form or other of service to the public. There are however a great many libraries and archives which have been created to serve a clearly defined group of people – a learned society, a trade or professional group, a religious denomination. Although these archives and libraries have as their primary purpose the information needs of their own members, they will very often be extremely helpful and receptive to requests for assistance from *bona fide* outside researchers. Because many of these institutions may have quite small staffs and have to prioritise service to their own members, it is generally wise to make the initial approach by mail or e-mail rather than turning up on their doorstep unannounced and asking for attention. A letter or e-mail also allows you to establish your credentials and confirm your seriousness of purpose; an appointment for a visit can then usually be made at a time convenient to you and the institution, or the information you want supplied in some other way.

So if the subject of your research was for example a lawyer, a doctor or an engineer, then it would be well worth investigating bodies such as the Law Society, the medical Royal Colleges, the Institution of Civil Engineers or the Institution of Mechanical Engineers. Remember also that in many fields, Scotland has retained and developed separate professional bodies and you might need to consult, for example, the Faculty of Advocates or the library of the Society of Writers to the Signet, or the Royal College of Surgeons of Edinburgh or the Royal College of Physicians and Surgeons of Glasgow.

Tracing which libraries and archive centres are likely to be relevant to your project can be difficult and often involves a fair degree of luck and perhaps some lateral thinking. However, there are a number of books that you should be able to find at your local reference library which can assist you in your initial search for sources:

Blatchford, Robert *ed.*: *Family and Local History Handbook*, 5th ed. York, The Genealogical Services Directory, 2001
Cox, Michael *ed.*: *Exploring Scottish History; with a directory of resource centres for Scottish local and national history in Scotland*, 2nd ed. Hamilton, Scottish Library Association, 1999

Dale, Peter *ed.*: *The Directory of Museums and Special Collections in the United Kingdom*, 2nd ed. London, ASLIB, 1996

Foster, J & Sheppard, J: *British Archives; a guide to archive resources in the United Kingdom*, 4th ed. Basingstoke, Palgrave, 2002

Record Repositories in Great Britain, 11th ed. London, PRO, 1999

Reynard, K W & Reynard, J M C: *The ASLIB Directory of Information Sources in the United Kingdom*, 10th ed. London, ASLIB, 1998

Reynard, K W: *Directory of Literary and Historical Collections in the United Kingdom*, London, ASLIB, 1993

National archives and libraries

The wealth of material that lies in local archives and libraries is truly impressive, and with any luck you will be able to find most of what you need there. However, some categories of records are held in the major national archive collections and you may need to travel to one of these in search of information. Again, the range of archival material they hold is enormous and it is hard to do more here than indicate some of the potential. Many of these archives – the Public Record Office (PRO) is an excellent example – produce a wide range of guides to help in the use of their collections, and these can be of great assistance in making the most productive use of a visit to the archive. For example the PRO has free leaflets available on their resources and research topics as diverse as British Army Officer Records for the First World War, Bankrupts and Insolvent Debtors 1710–1869, Merchant Shipping Crew Lists 1747–1860, or Passport Records.

In addition to these free leaflets the Public Record Office publishes a number of books giving greater detail on various areas of their collections and how they may be used for genealogical or biographical research. If the subject of your research falls into one of these areas, the PRO publications will suggest many fruitful lines of enquiry. Among the most useful titles are:

Fowler, S & Spencer, W: *Army Records for Family Historians*, 2nd ed. London, PRO, 1998

Kershaw, R: *Emigrants and Expats*, London, PRO, 2002

Kershaw, R & Pearsall, M: *Immigrants and Aliens*, London, PRO, 2000

Rodger, N A M: *Naval records for Genealogists*, 2nd ed. London, PRO, 1998

Scott, M: *Prerogative Court of Canterbury Wills and other Probate Records*, London, PRO, 1997

Shorney, D: *Protestant Non-Conformity and Roman Catholicism: a guide to sources in the Public Record Office*, London, PRO, 1996

Spencer, W: *Air Force Records for Family Historians*, London, PRO, 2000

Spencer, W: *Army Service Records of the First World War*, 3rd ed. London, PRO, 2001

The PRO and the Office for National Statistics (General Register Office) have made special provision for genealogists and family historians with the creation of the Family Records Centre (contact details in Chapter 12). This provides easy access to indexes of births, marriages and deaths in England and Wales since the start of civil registration in 1837, indexes of adoptions from 1927, Census returns for England and Wales from 1841 to 2001 and a range of other important sources. A useful companion guide to the Family Record Centre is Stella Colwell's *The Family Records Centre: a User's Guide* (2nd ed. London, PRO, 2002). Although the Family Records Centre was established to cater for people's huge interest in genealogy, it also provides an important resource for the biographer.

The state's bureaucracy has been so effective over the centuries that there is a very fair chance that your subject has entered into the official archives as a tax payer, a member of the armed services, a criminal, or in one of a hundred other ways. Nor is there any need for their contact with the state to have been particularly notable. For example, the PRO maintains a register of medals awarded to servicemen in the First World War: not just medals for gallantry or distinguished conduct, like the Victoria Cross or the Military Medal, but the campaign medals awarded for service in a particular theatre of operations – or just for being in the service, such as the commonly awarded trio for soldiers who served on the Western Front (the 1914–15

Star, the British War Medal and the Victory Medal). Although many First World War service records were destroyed – ironically enough by bombing in the Second World War – efforts are being made to supplement the existing records with material from other sources. You may be fortunate enough to find the service records and medical records, pension, disability and other documentation for very ordinary private soldiers.

'But in this world, nothing can be certain, except death and taxes.' So wrote Benjamin Franklin – and biographers can be duly grateful that when these certainties occur, some interesting and useful records are created. In England and Wales from 1796, death duties were charged on estates over a certain value. The PRO holds Death Duty Registers from 1796 to 1903 which are full of useful information on the deceased, their trustees and beneficiaries. Copies of these registers from 1796 to 1858 and their indexes from 1796 to 1903 are also available at the Family Records Centre. If the person you are interested in died after 1858 in England and Wales then there is a simple and efficient way of obtaining a copy of their will. For a fee, of £5.00 per item at the time of writing, the Probate Search Room at the Principal Registry of the Family Division of the High Court (for contact details, see Chapter 12) will produce a copy of all wills and administrations proved after 12th January 1858. Wills in England and Wales before that date were proved in a variety of church and other courts, and detailed information on these can be found in publications such as *Probate Jurisdictions: Where to Look for Wills* (J Gibson & E Churchill, Federation of Family History Societies, 5th ed., 2002). Many pre-1858 wills were proved in the Prerogative Court of Canterbury and microfilm copies of these records are also available at the Family Records Centre. In addition to this facility on-line access to over one million wills from the Prerogative Court of Canterbury dating from 1384 to 1858 is now available at www.documentsonline.pro.gov.uk. Searching this archive, using first and last names, place, date and occupation, is free and a digital transcript of the document can be downloaded for a fee of £3 per item.

Scottish wills (or 'testaments' as they were usually referred to in Scots law) may be searched for through the holdings of the National Archives of Scotland (for contact details, see Chapter 12). Until 1823 testaments were recorded in Commissary

Courts, which were roughly coterminous with the pre-Reformation dioceses of Scotland, and thereafter they were recorded in Sheriff Courts. It was normal to produce an inventory of the goods and assets of the deceased, so wills and testaments can be very revealing and useful documents – not only telling to whom the deceased left money, moveable property and land, but also giving a good picture of their wealth (or otherwise). The National Archives of Scotland also have extensive Registers of Deeds – these are extremely varied and include such biographically significant documents as marriage contracts, business partnership agreements, apprenticeship agreements and indeed any type of contractual undertaking which the parties had agreed to have recorded for preservation.

Researchers on Scottish subjects also have the advantage of a long-established and effective system of central recording of the transfer of lands. The Register of Sasines starts in 1599 and printed abridgements arranged by county, which provide key information sufficient for most biographical purposes, exist from 1781. Both the full documents and the abridgements, with indexes of persons and places, can be consulted at the National Archives of Scotland. This Register can be of great assistance in clarifying your subject's landholding – even down to the purchase of a single house. As loans secured on land or property were also recorded in the Register, a good picture of a person's financial dealings can be built up from this source.

A good overview of the types of records held by the National Archives of Scotland is provided by the Scottish Record Office's: *Guide to the National Archives of Scotland* (Edinburgh, The Stationery Office, 1996). A more general work which deals with the resources of both the National Archives of Scotland and those of New Register House – the location of the Registrar General for Scotland and the home of Scotland's archive of Old Parish Records, Civil Registration Records and Census returns – is Kathleen B Cory's *Tracing your Scottish Ancestry* (2nd ed., Edinburgh, Polygon, 2003). Like many works designed for the genealogist, Cory's book provides valuable guidance for the biographer.

There are many national museums and archives throughout the UK that may be of very great significance to the biographer, and full details of these are given in the reference works listed above. A few sample institutions might be worth mentioning simply to illustrate the range of such institutions and the resources they might be able to furnish. Full contact details for all of them are given in Chapter 12:

- British Library, Oriental and India Office Collection. Holds the archives of the former East India Company and the India Office. Among its resources are registers of the names of applicants for those seeking employment with the East India Company and the Government of India (1771–1946) and lists of the European residents of the Presidencies of Bengal, Madras and Bombay (1702–1830)
- British Library, Manuscripts Department. A major collection of manuscripts, particularly strong in archival holdings of literary and political figures.
- Imperial War Museum. The history of modern war, and people's experience of war and wartime life in Britain and the Commonwealth. Extensive photographic collections.
- National Army Museum. Tells the story of British land forces from the 15th century to the present day, and the history of Commonwealth land forces up to their respective dates of independence. Whilst the Museum is an excellent place to find out about the general history of the Army, it holds few official records, and is unlikely to be able to provide information on individual soldiers.
- National Maritime Museum. Over four and a half miles of manuscripts including Admiralty and dockyard records, the business papers of shipping companies and other non-governmental organisations.
- National Monuments Record. Ten million items covering England's buildings, archaeology and maritime sites. The collections include: three million photographs, dating from the 1860s to the present day, of England's buildings; survey reports on specific buildings and archaeological sites; a complete set of listed building descriptions for England; and data on most known English archaeological sites.
- Royal Commission on Ancient and Historical Monuments of Scotland. Holds the National Monuments Record of Scotland – the national collection of material relating to the archaeological and architectural heritage of Scotland. Users of its

services include students, authors, academics, architects, planners, picture researchers, local historians, television and film producers, genealogists and social historians.

- National War Museum of Scotland. The Museum explores the Scottish experience of war and military service over the last 400 years. Its document collection encompasses a wide range of material from single personal items, such as letters and diaries, to large collections of official or semi-official papers.
- Public Record Office of Northern Ireland. Extensive collections of official archives, wills and testaments, church, estate and genealogical sources.
- National Library of Wales. Although much Welsh material is located in the Public Record Office, the National Library of Wales holds substantial archival deposits.

Increasingly, a great deal of research can be done online by means of a computer at home or in a local access point such as a public library. All public library services are currently being connected to the Internet through the People's Network project and will offer free Internet access.

Online sources

All the major national archives, and many local archives, have already put online a considerable quantity both of primary source material and of finding aids such as catalogues, and there is a general commitment to increase this. Of course the day is unlikely to come when every document you might wish to see is available online – the quantity of material, the limited demand for so much of it and the rate of addition of archive materials all makes this impracticable. However, a worthwhile amount of fascinating material is already accessible through computer links and a lot of emphasis has gone into producing learning resources for both formal and informal education. For the researcher, the new facility of online access to catalogues, lists and finding aids is perhaps more significant than the availability of digitised copies of highlights from these collections.

The digital collections and information offered by national and local archives and museums have the great advantage of being quality assured – something that cannot be claimed for much material found on the Internet. Use of the Internet search engines such as http://uk.altavista.com or http://www.google.com can produce fascinating and valuable information about people and things of interest; however, in the absence of the stamp of authority given by the *imprimatur* of a reputable national agency such as the Imperial War Museum, it is often hard to determine whether this information is accurate, when it was last revised, what the source is, and whether the material on the website has been legitimately obtained and does not infringe copyright. (For information on copyright matters, see Chapter 9.) Sadly, this is as true of some authoritative-looking sites as it is of amateur ones. One educational website I consulted in search of information on a Scottish politician and lawyer suggested that he died in 1965 at the age of 102 – which, while not impossible, was perhaps slightly unlikely. On closer examination the page said that the man was born in 1863 and that he became a solicitor at the age of 41 in 1904, which seemed suspiciously late in life to enter on such a career. Reliable evidence was later found to indicate a birth date of 1879, making qualification as a solicitor at the age of 25 a more probable event, and his death to have occurred at the age of 86 in 1965. Evidence, from whatever source, needs to be weighed and evaluated and tested against probability and other sources. Sadly, although the Internet offers many wonderful resources, it also offers a great deal of secondhand, inadequately researched and incompetently presented material.

All the more reason to welcome the advent of co-operative projects such as SCAN and A2A which draw on a wide range of resources to create high-quality specimen materials, interpretative materials and finding aids. These projects are incomplete – indeed by their very nature they may never be complete – but already provide an extremely valuable resource:

- SCAN – the Scottish Archives Network. It aims to convert the top-level catalogues of 50 Scottish archives into electronic format and make these available via the Internet, allowing users worldwide to find out which records are held where in Scotland. Also to make a major historical resource, the wills and testaments of Scots from 1500–1875, available to researchers worldwide. This latter project is now available at http://www.scottishdocuments.com. The SCAN service can be accessed at http://www.scan.org.uk.

- A2A – the Access to Archives Project. The English strand of the UK Archives network, in March 2003 A2A had placed online more than 4.35 million catalogue entries from 318 archives and other repositories. This database demonstrates the ease and simplicity with which multiple archive searches can now be conducted. A specimen search on Rudyard Kipling produced 51 hits in 35 archives or archive collections. While some of these would have been found fairly easily by traditional search methods, others may not have been discovered without a computer search. For example, the two documents in the Baldwin papers in Worcestershire Records Office would probably have been traced by a diligent researcher (Kipling was a cousin of Prime Minister Stanley Baldwin, so a Baldwin archive would be a fairly natural place to look). Others, though – like the letter by Kipling declining to write a foreword to a book by General Maurice, which is in the Liddell Hart Centre for Military Archives in King's College London – might have remained hidden. As A2A and other access databases grow and develop they will become increasingly valuable, offering the researcher a seamless access to national and local archives. A2A can be accessed at http://www.a2a.org.uk.

- The National Register of Archives. Contains information on the nature and location of manuscripts and historical records that relate to British history. The NRA is maintained by the Historical Manuscripts Commission and allows a search of the holdings of a very wide range of archives, including the major national collections. However, it does provide less detailed information than the A2A project. It has the advantage of covering archive depositories across the UK as well as listing UK material in foreign archives, and although the online information is limited the full catalogues of the NRA are available in their search rooms and in the major national archives. The NRA can be accessed at http://www.hmc.gov.uk/nra.

Services like the NRA and A2A are complementary. A check on Rudyard Kipling in the NRA produced 40 locations of Kipling archival material, ranging from the National Library of Australia through the Kipling Society to Harvard University Library and the Bodleian Library, Oxford. There was surprisingly little overlap with the locations returned by an A2A search, although the A2A entries yielded information on individual documents – such as dates of letters – while the NRA entries gave information at collection level, such as name of collection, address of archive, opening times, facilities, etc. A thorough search would need to employ both types of resource – and both sites give links to other specialised search facilities.

One (perhaps obvious) point about using any of these databases is that unless you are very fortunate, you will encounter entries for people with the same name as your subject but who are totally unrelated. While writing this chapter I did a search on A2A for one of my own research interests, the 19th century Clyde shipbuilder and marine engineer, Robert Napier (1791–1876). I was impressed to find hits in 39 different catalogues under this name; a result I thought quite remarkable bearing in mind that A2A only covers English archives and my subject lived and worked in Scotland – although he was heavily involved in Admiralty and East India Company contracts. However, closer examination of the hits showed that the vast majority of these results referred to the quite unrelated Victorian General, Robert Napier, 1st Baron Napier of Magdala (1810–1890). The construction of these search engines also means that a search on Robert Napier will return an entry where it occurs as part of a longer name – such as Robert Napier Smith. So check carefully to ensure that you are in fact finding sources relevant to your subject. Most of the time a bit of common sense and the context of the collection should make this clear: for example the catalogue entry from the Institution of Mechanical Engineers is more likely to refer to 'my' Robert Napier, and the one from the House of Lords Record Office to Lord Napier of Magdala. If the information on the catalogue record does not make things clear then a preliminary enquiry to the archive may save a wasted journey. The A2A site provides contact details for each of the archives included.

The NRA site also has a useful 'Archives in Focus' feature offering helpful advice to beginners, with sections on what archives are and how they might be of use to you, and on the use of archives in popular fields such as family and local history.

There are many significant online sources offering access to vital records information. One of the most useful of these is the Family Search Internet Genealogy Service run by the Mormons (or the Church of Jesus Christ of Latter-day Saints). The Mormon Church places an emphasis on genealogy as a means of bringing believers' ancestors within the scope of the Church; to assist in this it has undertaken massive projects to transcribe birth, marriage and death records from around the world. The by-product of this has been a number of extremely useful products for genealogists and other researchers. While there are deficiencies at times in their transcription, and some evidence of wishful thinking in asserting familial links where these cannot, in fact, be proved, the database offers an easy and entirely free way of establishing basic information about people you wish to research. It can be accessed at http://www.familysearch.org.

The Mormons have also made available some useful CD-ROMs – for example, transcriptions of the enumerators' books for the 1881 UK Census – at astonishingly low prices. At the time of writing, the 25 discs of the Census are available for around £30 and represent an extremely worthwhile research tool for anyone doing biographical research around that period. A census entry will show the family structure and the names and relationship of any non-family members present on Census day – servants, visitors, etc. – as well as indicating age, place of birth, and occupation. You can also find out who the neighbours of your subject were – a piece of information that can be extremely helpful and may answer many questions besides giving a useful indication of the socio-economic status of the area in which your subject lived. The Church also maintains a series of Family History Centres throughout the country where such products can be used and online sources accessed.

Earlier in this chapter the availability of printed indexes to newspapers was noted. While these can be very useful, they do tend to suffer from the handicap of a limited number of index terms being selected for each item, as well as an almost inevitable inconsistency in the choice of terms used over time. At its simplest this can mean that at any one time, a particular newspaper indexes deaths by providing an alphabetical list of names under D for Deaths, and at another time under O for

Obituaries; and then changes to indexing obituaries primarily by the surname of the deceased person. Preferred names of organisations, institutions and concepts change and the European War becomes the World War, becomes the Great War, becomes the First World War. The computer age, and with it the possibility of digitally scanning newspapers, providing free-text searching and delivering this over the Internet, has made archive newspapers a much more accessible resource for the researcher. Among the leading examples of this is *The Times Digital Archive*, a full-image online archive of every page published by *The Times* [London] from 1785 to 1985. The text within the images is fully searchable at the article level; users can easily search news articles, obituaries, advertising and classifieds – indeed, virtually everything that appeared in the newspaper. Results are displayed at the article level; and users may view either the article, or the full page upon which it appeared. The free-text searching means that even the most passing reference to a topic or person of interest will be captured and displayed, with, of course, certain consequent hazards. It is not until you actually use such a resource that you realise exactly how vague language can be. Searching for information on a man called Derby will produce hits for the town and county of Derby, the classic horserace, the cabinet ministers the 14th & 15th Earls of Derby, and doubtless a type of gentleman's hat too. Precision in the use of search terms and some thought on search strategies is essential if you are not to be swamped by unwanted references. If the object of your research is called Smith and lived in London then perhaps a search under some other term – such as an occupation or some distinctive word associated with him – would be more useful. *The Times Digital Archive* is available online at subscribing libraries.

One other facility offered by the Internet is worth investigating. It carries thousands of online discussion boards and mailing lists on every conceivable subject, and an appeal for assistance on an appropriate board or list may prove to be a very fruitful source of information. Of course, like all other forms of information, the source needs to be considered, its reliability assessed and the material obtained evaluated against other sources. A search on http://www.google.com or http://uk.altavista.com will produce relevant lists, or you could consult http://www.lsoft.com/lists.listref.html which offers details of

71,488 publicly available lists. Many of the people who use these lists are both helpful and knowledgeable and represent a valuable and often overlooked resource. Bear in mind that, like all co-operative ventures, these lists and discussion boards are only as good as the contributory parts – so if you can help an enquirer with something from your own area of expertise, then be sure to do so. Casting your bread on the water comes highly recommended!

There are a great many websites which list people who have emigrated from the UK, for example to Australia, Canada or New Zealand. One particularly rich site has made available the millions of immigration records from Ellis Island, New York from 1892 to 1924. The entry manifests compiled by the shipping lines and checked by the US Customs and Immigration staff have been digitised and can be searched online free of charge. Not only does this site allow you to find when and from which ship a person entered the United States, it also has details of their occupation, nationality, ethnicity, place of origin, reason for coming to the United States, contacts within the United States, ability to read and write, height, distinguishing characteristics, etc. Thus we find the novelist Joseph Conrad landing in the USA on 1st May 1923, having sailed from Glasgow on the liner *Tuscania*. We learn that his contact in the States was Frank Doubleday of Oyster Beach, New York [his US publisher], that Conrad was 5 feet 9 inches tall, of florid complexion with dark brown hair and brown eyes, had £80 of cash with him, paid his own fare and was neither a polygamist nor an anarchist nor was he intending to overthrow by force or violence the government of the United States. Reassuringly he was declared to be capable of reading and writing English, was a British citizen and had been born in Gitomir, Poland and that this was his first visit to the United States. Similar records can be found for 22 million other visitors, emigrants and merchant seamen who passed through Ellis Island. The site can be accessed at http://www.ellisisland.org.

Personal contacts

While always making the most of printed reference sources and manuscript archives, and exploring online access to databases and search engines to the full, the biographer should never over-look the value of personal contact. Even for long-dead subjects, talking to other researchers and enthusiasts can be immensely valuable in providing you with insights and helping you trace sources. However shy you might be about announcing that you are writing a biography of X or Y, it is probably well worth mentioning it to anybody you think might be interested or help-ful. I have had many good leads as a result of talking about projects to friends and acquaintances, and have found other researchers to be extremely generous about sharing information and documents. Of course there is a chance that you will come across somebody who is researching the same subject as you with a view to writing a biography – and this has happened to me on a couple of occasions. However, it is always as well to know, at an early stage, that competitors exist. All you can do is decide whether the world needs or can use two biographies of the same person, and act accordingly. In one such case I decided that the other author was much better qualified to write the book than I was and abandoned the project, fortunately before having spent too much time and effort on the idea. In the second case the other author, who had been planning to write about a subject I was well advanced on, decided to leave the field to me. Moreover he was able to supply me with copies of some inter-esting documents and later arranged a local radio interview for me when my book was published. In the first case I found out about the other author through the descendant of my proposed subject, whom I had contacted to seek his cooperation in the project. In the second, I answered the other author's request for information on an Internet discussion board. In both cases a positive result emerged from being open about my project and talking as widely as possible about it.

It is always hard to know what descendants of your subject may have that could assist you in your project. Sometimes noth-ing, except perhaps family traditions and legends; sometimes invaluable material that will never find its way into archives and museums. It is certainly worth making the effort to find out – although this can be difficult at times. If you are working on the type of subject who features in *Burke's Peerage* then the process is reasonably straightforward, but otherwise you may have to work a little harder at it. A letter in a local paper or magazine circulating in the area where your subject lived might produce a response, either from a descendant or from somebody who can provide further leads.

There are many ways of tracing people who could be useful to you as you research and write your project. It is a fairly good bet that somebody who has written a book on, say, a fighter ace in the First World War, will have some valuable suggestions to make about contacts and sources for the biography of another fighter pilot. You will generally find a very positive response to this sort of enquiry, people with expertise usually are happy to talk about their area of knowledge and share their experience with other interested people. Of course such help needs to be properly acknowledged in your published work and needs to be sought with a degree of sensitivity. If the other author is writing a series of books about First World War fighter pilots it is hardly reasonable to expect him to assist a competitor. In most cases a little research will indicate what the situation is.

Another way of finding contacts and using other people's expertise is to check and see if there is a society, trade or professional body active in the field of your interest, and contact them. Try an Internet search, or consult one of the printed listings such as Henderson, S P A & Henderson, A J W *eds.*: *Directory of British Associations and Associations in Ireland*, 14th ed. Beckenham, CBD Research Ltd, 1998 or Sheets, Tara *ed.*: *Trade Associations and Professional Bodies of the United Kingdom and Eire*, 11th ed. London, Graham & Whiteside, 2001. Such works are also compiled for smaller areas, an example being – Baird, W W & Whittles, K H *eds.*: *Directory of Scotland's Organisations*, Latheronwheel (Caithness), Whittles Publishing, 1998.

For literary subjects there is a useful website – maintained jointly by the Harry Ransom Humanities Research Center at the University of Texas at Austin, and the University of Reading Library – called WATCH. Standing for Writers, Artists and their Copyright Holders, this was established to provide an efficient way of obtaining copyright clearance for writers and artists whose archives are held in whole or in part by institutions in the United States and the United Kingdom. However, it does offer the opportunity to trace relatives or legal representatives of dead authors and artists.

Interviewing

If your biography is of a living person, then you will almost certainly have to interview not just your subject, but also their relatives, friends, acquaintances, 'enemies' and colleagues. This can be quite a daunting prospect and some thought needs to be given to what you want from the interview, how you might conduct it, how long it might last, where it will take place and how you are going to record it. After all, you are asking somebody to give up what might be quite a lot of their time to talk to you, and perhaps to go into matters that are in some ways sensitive, so you owe it to them to be as well prepared for the interview as possible, to conduct it in the most professional way and to accurately represent their views. This does not of course mean that you have to agree with them, nor that you should suspend your critical faculties. Although the person you are interviewing may have lived through a particular event, you cannot assume that their recollection of it is accurate, that their knowledge of it was comprehensive, or, indeed, that they are not deliberately telling you lies. The better prepared you are before the interview, the better able you will be to assess what you are being told, and the better equipped you will be to keep the conversation on productive lines.

Before you set up the interview, agree the areas to be discussed; this is both courteous and useful, as it gives your interviewee an opportunity to marshal their thoughts, perhaps look out papers, and refresh their memory. It is wise not to plan to do too much in one session, and important to watch out for signs that your interviewee is tiring or getting nervous or unhappy. Better to wind things up smoothly and arrange another session than to push on and perhaps lose a valuable contact or alienate an important source.

The setting for your interview is important. The person you are talking to may feel more comfortable on their own territory, but if the conversation is going to be regularly interrupted (by children needing food, dogs needing water or doors needing answering) it can be very distracting, and it might be worth thinking about another setting – your home, or a neutral location like a hotel. Interviews usually work best with just you and the interviewee, but in some cases it might be necessary to have a third party present – a friend or a relative to give the person you are talking to confidence, or to help them if there are difficulties over language. Make sure however that you are getting your evidence from the prime source, and not moderated or modified by the helpful friend.

A list of questions that you want answered is a useful preliminary, and you might find it useful to supply this in advance to the person you are going to interview. Avoid becoming so fixated on ticking off answers on your list that you cannot follow your contact into interesting areas. The advantage of the interview as a research tool is that it can open up fields that you might never have known about or thought of – so don't lose this advantage by sticking too rigidly to a pre-arranged plan.

You may at times need to 'challenge' your interviewee – if, for example, what they are telling you appears to contradict other, reliable, information you already have. It is important to test what you are being told, but it is even more important to do it in a way that is non-confrontational and unaggressive. It is usually possible to find an acceptable way of doing this and the resulting discussion can often prove to be particularly useful and revealing.

Unless you are gifted with total recall, you will have to consider how you are going to record your conversation. There is no doubt that a tape recording is the easiest and simplest method, and inexpensive portable recorders made for office dictation purposes can be perfectly adequate (there is no need for studio-quality recording, just for a clear sound quality). These machines generally have a built-in microphone and, if placed on a table between you and the person you are interviewing, should pick up both voices quite satisfactorily – although a separate microphone will usually give somewhat better results. A trial run to judge what recording level is needed, and what the best position might be is a sensible precaution – and make sure that you have spare batteries and enough tape cassettes to last the session! Recently, digital recorders have come on the market offering longer recording times and the ability to transfer the files via a USB port to your computer for later transcription, storage or transmission via email. Whatever system you use, make quite sure you know how to work the machine: quiet confidence in your equipment builds up trust on the part of the interviewee; a desperate scrambling to push the right buttons, or a horrified realisation that the record button has not been pushed on and the last half hour has been wasted, does not do much to convince the interviewee that you are a serious professional worth devoting time and effort to.

If you do decide to use a tape recorder, give some extra thought to the location of your interview – a quiet area is needed. Try to avoid echoing rooms; the microphone has a way of emphasising any odd acoustics which makes later playback and transcription very difficult. I once interviewed somebody in a works canteen and, quite apart from regular door banging as people came in and out for their tea, the hard surfaces and echoing atmosphere made the recording almost unusable.

As well as helping you to represent the interviewee's words correctly, a recorder enables you to concentrate on what you are being told rather than worrying about scribbling it down. Unfortunately, some people are more reluctant to talk to a tape recorder than to an interviewer armed only with a notepad; but the benefits of recording your interview do make it worthwhile trying to persuade a reluctant person to consent to it – particularly if a small, non-threatening dictation machine is being used. Finally, if you end up doing a lot of recorded interviews, do make sure that you clearly identify which source is which and when the interview was conducted. When it is transcribed, you may want to consider letting your interviewee see the draft – and certainly this is important if you have made notes rather than taken an audio recording. Sight of the transcript gives them confidence that they have not been misrepresented, and may also spark off further memories or produce corrections or amplifications.

If you are going to do much interviewing, you might profitably look at one of the books on the techniques of oral history – such as Stephen Caunce's *Oral History and the Local Historian* (London, Longman, 1994) or Paul Thompson's *The Voice of the Past: Oral History* (Oxford, OUP, 2000). You could also read the information on oral history techniques available on the Internet, such as www.indiana.edu/~ohrc/pamph1.htm.

Visiting places – recording and photographing

One of the key areas of biographical research is also, to me, one of the most fascinating and attractive – the search for buildings, sites and locations associated with your subject. There are two main reasons for visiting such places: one is that in a rather strange way, walking in your subject's footsteps brings you closer to them and may often make many things about them much clearer. The other is that, sometimes, you will be fortunate enough to find hard evidence that has otherwise eluded you.

It is always worthwhile visiting places associated with your subject, and this is particularly true if their house still exists or a grave can be found, a memorial brass or window in a church discovered, or indeed any tangible evidence unearthed. It is even worth doing where your subject left no visible trace but simply passed through a landscape, for it can be immensely valuable to see things through the subject's eyes. A fine explanation of this doctrine comes in Richard Holmes' *Footsteps, Adventures of a Romantic Biographer*. In this subtle and fascinating book, the author travels for example in the French Cevennes in the track of Robert Louis Stevenson, and writes that:

> The past does retain a physical presence for the biographer – in landscapes, buildings, photographs, and above all the actual trace of handwriting on original letters and journals.*

The importance of exploring a subject's physical environment was twice brought home to me in one day when I was researching Alasdair Macdonell of Glengarry. I knew he was buried in a family mausoleum some 20 miles from his Inverness-shire home – so I went to visit it. The most significant thing in the mausoleum was that while there were elaborate carved tombstones for his ancestors, there was no stone for him. Given that he died in 1828 with debts of £80,000, this lack of elaborate funerary monument may be thought unsurprising but it did vividly underline, and physically embody, the decline in his family fortunes.

*Holmes, Richard: *Footsteps, Adventures of a Romantic Biographer*, London, Flamingo, 1995 (p. 67)

A few miles on from the mausoleum, I was passing through the small village of Laggan when I saw a sign pointing to a church where no church appeared to be. My curiosity aroused, I walked down a grassy lane and found a small, very plain, 19th century church-like building with no sign to indicate its name or denomination. Asking for information at a nearby house I was told it was a chapel that had been built for workers on the adjacent Caledonian Canal. I recollected that I had seen a reference to Macdonell building a chapel for Episcopalian worship somewhere in this area, and hoped this was the one. I found out where the keys for the building were kept, got them and went in.

Inside, the church was even plainer and shabbier than it was outside. There was only one object of any interest – an elaborate marble slab with the names and dates of birth and death of six young male children, inscribed 'By an affectionate father erected to the memory of his sons'. There was no surname given but the Christian names and dates confirmed that these were six sons of Alasdair Macdonell – all of whom had died in the first year of life. This memorial not only gave me a very moving connection to my subject – and a vivid and tangible reminder of a real and recurrent tragedy in his life – but it was actually the only reliable evidence I was ever able to uncover for the names and dates of birth and death of a number of these boys (the church records being defective, civil registration not yet being required, and previous clan and family histories being inaccurate or incomplete).

When you are doing these field trips it is always a good idea to record what you find. Take notes, take photographs, take video film. Even if you feel that the photographs are not likely to be of sufficiently high quality for publication, a file of pictures forms an excellent aid to memory and is a good stimulus for your imagination. Photographs will also be useful if, as will surely be the case, you are asked to speak about your book. If you take your photographs as prints, it is possible to have these copied on to transparencies for slide projection – or you may consider using them in digital form for a PowerPoint type of presentation. In any event a photographic record of scenes, buildings, sites and locations associated with your research is a valuable asset.

Luck!

When all the sources that you can think of for your biography have been explored, the last archive visited, the most obscure Internet site explored, the remotest personal contact followed up, then there is still the matter of luck. One delightful example of luck is recounted by William Dalrymple in his captivating book *White Mughals*.* Dalrymple had spent five years researching the remarkable, and largely unknown, love story of the marriage of James Achilles Kirkpatrick, the British Resident at the Court of Hyderabad at the end of the 18th century, to a Mughal lady of high birth, Khair-un-Nissa. On the last day of his third and last visit to Hyderabad, having spent several months working in various archives in the city and with just a few hours to spare before catching his flight to Delhi and then home to the UK, he realised that he had failed to buy any presents for his family. He went into the market to look for a local speciality, a Bidri decorated metalwork box. A boy offered to take him to a shop that sold 'booxies'. The shop proved to sell not boxes but books – or rather manuscripts bought up from Hyderabadi palaces. Dalrymple told the owner what he was working on, and found to his astonishment that he produced, among other treasures, a 600-page autobiography written by Khair-un-Nissa's cousin. He concludes his account of this incident: 'I spent the rest of the afternoon haggling with the owner, and left his shop £400 poorer, but with a trunkload of previously untranslated primary sources. Their contents completely transformed what followed.'

Few of us, perhaps, will ever have quite such a remarkable find, but Dalrymple's experience underlines the importance of luck, of talking about your research to anybody who might conceivably be able to help, and having the intellectual honesty to follow new evidence wherever it takes you.

---

*Dalrymple, William: *White Mughals, Love and Betrayal in Eighteenth-century India*, London, Flamingo, 2002 (pp. x1iii–x1iv)

7

Organising Your Information

You have at last traced the documents you want to look at; you have arrived at the record office with your pencils sharpened; and the documents, which have been brought up from the store, are lying before you on your desk. So what now?

Your time is precious – you might have travelled hundreds or even thousands of miles to see these documents. So how can you employ this time efficiently, how can you be sure that you are making the best use of the documents, and how do you ensure that you extract everything necessary from them? How can you avoid the irritating and perhaps expensive necessity of re-visiting this archive and re-reading these papers?

Be thoroughly prepared – read, summarise and select

Part of the answer lies in preparation. If you arrive at a record office or library 'cold', not knowing what sort of documents you will be using or much about their background, then it is likely that at a first reading you will miss a lot of what they contain and fail to pick up on some quite significant things. To take a simple example: the person you are researching was a nurse in a military hospital on the Western Front in the First World War, and you have traced a bundle of her letters home in a County Record Office. If you are not familiar with the background – the history of the war, the organisation of military hospitals, the writer's family – then it is almost certain that the letters will contain allusions to people, places and organisations that may confuse you. Does a reference to 'French' mean the inhabitants of France or the British commander-in-chief Field Marshal French; is 'Big Bertha' another nurse or a heavy German siege gun?

These are simple enough examples and the context should provide you with clues – but other references, such as use of military abbreviations or once common colloquialisms, are likely to be considerably more difficult.

So reading yourself into a subject is essential – even if you cannot wait to get to grips with the documents. There is little worse than realising afterwards that something you failed to make a note of, because you were sure it was of little significance, has now taken on a new importance – perhaps because your growing familiarity with the subject has allowed you to put it into its proper context and to value it accordingly. Realising too late that there was something interesting, or a quotation that would make your point wonderfully well, in an archive source you used six months ago is deeply frustrating. I know, because I have been in that position!

Considering what sort of information you might want to extract from the documents is another essential preliminary. If you know you will need to extract a lot of repetitive information, such as occupations from census returns, or ages from death records, then it is well worth taking the time to prepare some form of data sheet before your visit so that you can maximise the value of your time with the documents. If you prepare a sheet that only needs ticks or figures inserted then you can process a great many more pages than if you had to write everything down. Think too about the sort of abbreviations you can use (but do be sure that you note down what the abbreviations stand for! Of course you will understand that ingenious abbreviation today, but next month or next year it may be utterly baffling).

When you are faced with documents your natural instinct is to start reading them immediately. However, it is worth taking a few minutes just to get a feel for them and to ask – and possibly find answers to – a few important questions which may not be apparent from the description or catalogue record:

- What period do they cover, and do they seem complete for that period?
- Is there any indication of how they came to be in this particular record office or library?
- Is there any significance in their physical condition?

- Why were they written?
- Are there any aids to help you get the best use out of the documents?

Answers to these questions can help you to get the most out of the records, and indeed can often point you to other areas of research. For example, a gap in a diary may be evidence that the writer was unable to find time to write it up during that period. Can you find out why? A physical gap – pages missing – may suggest suppression of information by the writer or by a later custodian.

The source of the records can provide valuable, indeed irreplaceable, clues. Official documents arrive at record offices by a variety of generally understandable routes, but private gifts and deposits can be much more interesting and revealing. Details of the donor are usually available and may give you leads for further investigations – why did that person have possession of these letters or this diary? What was the connection between the donor and the author? Is there somebody still living whom you can contact?

The physical condition of the documents is also of some significance – and can at times be a vitally important clue. A deeply creased letter showing signs of being read and re-read, folded and unfolded time after time, has quite a different character and tells a different story from that of a pristine document which has been read once and filed. And the reason *why* a record was created is always a crucial question. As was discussed in Chapter 1, a document is seldom if ever created to help us write biographies, and we need to establish its original purpose and think about possible bias, error or unreliability.

You will find that some records have already been transcribed in full or summarised, and this can save you a great deal of work. Check very simple things – for example, look and see if there is an index to the document. I once spent an hour reading through a thick handwritten volume of legal records trying to find a reference to somebody I was working on, only to find, when I had completed my task, that there was an extremely full index to the volume at the end.

As you read through a document, consider how much of it you are going to use and how you are going to copy it. To some extent your decision on this will be governed by the nature of the collection of archives and the scale of the documents. If a packet of four letters is all that you have been able to trace relating to your subject, then you may feel that it would be simplest just to have them photocopied. They will then be available for you to consult and use at any time. If on the other hand your subject is one of those people who seemed to do nothing but write letters, it may be economically impossible to have everything copied – and in any case you may feel that most of the letters are of little real significance.

The question of how you will integrate archive material into your finished work is something that we will come on to in Chapter 8, but however you decide to use it there is no doubt that quoting from original sources gives your narrative a liveliness and a directness, as well as adding authenticity and reliability. You will certainly want to have the exact words of a document available for use on many occasions. In the case of most documents you will read them, make a précis of them, and perhaps transcribe or have photocopied any particularly significant passage or passages for which you need a detailed record or which you think would be quotable. These decisions are often quite difficult and there is always a terrible temptation to copy everything, just to be 'on the safe-side'. However, this can be very time-consuming and, if you have to get copying done, quite expensive. Many archives do not allow you to use self-service copiers, and charges for copying done by the archive staff – which usually costs several times the price of coin-in-the-slot copying – can soon mount up. Frequently, too, the format of a particular document does not make for cheap copying and the archive's conservation requirements may mean that a more expensive type of copy has to be ordered.

It is also true to say that the discipline of reading, summarising and selecting does ensure that the full meaning of a document is absorbed and mastered. Photocopiers have certainly made our lives much easier, but information can pass all too quickly from a document to a photocopy and into your file without ever really passing through your brain. Of course there will always be documents of which you simply must have a full copy available, but often there is no real need for you to have every last dot and comma.

Taking notes

What you *do* need is a very reliable, legible and understandable note. I have found that my handwriting, which starts out as quite reasonable at 9.00 a.m., is barely legible after a long day in an archive and a week later is a profound mystery to me. Now I tend to use a laptop computer to take my notes – I can type just about as quickly as I can write and I have a permanently legible record which can, of course, be cut and pasted into my final text without any additional work. Most libraries and archives have now come to grips with the idea of the laptop computer: many, such as the Public Record Office, have designated areas for computer users, where the click of keys will not interfere with the concentration of those using the more silent and traditional technology of pencil and paper. Most, though not all, have power points. Some will still ask you to fill in a form indemnifying the institution against various improbable eventualities.

However you decide to take your notes, there are some essentials that you should record:

- The source of the information. This will be needed for the purposes of providing references and citations, and if you subsequently decide that you need to obtain a copy of the document or to source an illustration. This information should indicate:
  - The library or record office, e.g. British Library
  - If it is from a named collection within that institution, e.g. Liverpool Papers
  - The name of, or type of, document, e.g. Muster Roll, Letter book, Correspondence
  - The piece number, e.g. Add Mss 38249
  - The page number(s), if any, e.g. f123. Collections of letters, etc. are either bound or held in folders and conventionally have 'f' (for folio numbers) given to each sheet – thus f123 is page 123 and ff 123–5 are pages 123 to 125. In some cases the reverse side of a page will be referred to as f123 v (for verso). These folio numbers have usually been pencilled on to the document by the archivist. As a folder or binder of letters may contain several hundred pages, the folio number is essential for accurate referencing

- The date of the document.
- The author of the document. The address from which the document, for example a letter, was written can often prove to be significant and is always worth noting – although if 99% of the letters are written from the same address you will undoubtedly want to find some shorthand method of indicating this (or simply note the exceptions).
- The person to whom the document is addressed or for whom it was intended. Remember that the style of salutation and closure may be important – see Chapter 1, pp. 10–11. There is a great deal of difference between a letter which starts 'Dear Winston' and one which starts 'Dear Prime Minister'; and between one which ends 'Yours respectfully, Jean Smith (Mrs.)' and one which ends 'Much love, Tiddles'. If there seems to be some significance in this area, make a note.
- A brief description of the document.
- A summary of the contents or a complete or partial transcript.

References and citations

You will want to be able to cite the sources that you have used for direct quotation, whether these are previous books or articles, or original archival materials. There are two reasons for this: to allow other researchers to validate your work and your conclusions, and to give due credit to previous writers' work so that you avoid accusations of plagiarism. There are a number of ways of providing references and citations, and if you have a publisher for your work you may find that they expect you to conform to a house style. If this is not the case then you have some more freedom. Any referencing system must be simple, clearly understood and unambiguous; if it also looks reasonably attractive, then that is an added advantage.

In the field of providing references, fashions have changed: once, the normal method was to include a footnote – that is, a piece of quoted text or reference identified by a superscript number such as [17] or a conventional symbol such as †, ‡, or ¶. The same number was repeated at the foot of the page, with the full details of the source:

[17] Osborne, B D: *The Last of the Chiefs*, 2001, p. 127
¶ Public Record Office: CAB120/363 Weapons: Anti-Aircraft Guns: UP weapons

This method is useful in that it allows for the easiest form of reference to the source, but it can make for a rather untidy page – particularly if there are a great many citations. It also sometimes results in there being more text in footnotes than in the main part of the page.

An alternative to footnotes now is endnotes – that is, gathering all the references together at the end of a chapter, or more usually nowadays, at the end of the book. This latter position tends to be favoured by publishers, not least because it is the most economical in terms of space; chapter endnotes are probably easier for the reader to use as they are closer to the text. Conventional symbols do not work when there are more than five or six references, and superscript numbers are now almost always used instead. These can be continuous throughout the book, but more commonly a new sequence is started for each chapter – especially if there are a great many references to be cited, since three-digit superscript numbers do tend to be rather off-putting.

In the academic world an alternative form of referencing – the Harvard Convention – has evolved. This is particularly useful where repeated citation is being made of a published book or journal article, as its details need only to be given once in a consolidated list of works cited at the end of the text. The Harvard Convention works both for reference to published works and when quoting text from such a work. The surname of the author or authors and the year of publication are given in brackets at the appropriate place in the text (the year of publication distinguishes between different works of the same author – if there is more than one book by the same author published in the same year, deal with it by adding a letter after the date). Examples of the use of the Harvard Convention might be:

As has been pointed out, the steamboat was not a new invention in 1812 (Osborne, 1995)

or for a direct quotation

'Bell was by no means the first to try to make a practical and commercial success of steam navigation' (Osborne, 1995, p. 15)

Where there are two authors, both are normally given – e.g. MacGibbon & Ross, 1896. Where there are more than two, the Latin abbreviation *et al* (and others) is used – e.g. Jenkinson *et al*, 2001. The list of sources to which these references point should be formatted in alphabetical order in the following sequence: Author(s), Date of Publication, Title of Book (and number of edition if later than 1st), and Publisher. For journal articles much the same sequence is used: Author(s), Date of Publication, Title of Article, Name of Journal, Volume or Issue number, Page number(s).

The choice of system may come down to a matter of taste. Personally I prefer the endnote system to the Harvard Convention, because I think it tends to work better for the type of citation you are likely to be using in biographical writing – particularly if there are numerous references to archival materials.

Quite how much information you need to give in an endnote reference is again debatable. Reference to manuscripts should be as precise as possible and should conform to the points made earlier. References to published works certainly need to have the author's last name and forename or initials and the title of the work. It used to be conventional to cite in full the place of publication, publisher and date of publication (Frankfurt am Main, Peter Lang GmbH, 1996) but increasingly this tends to be somewhat simplified – except in very formal works, such as doctoral theses – and quite often either the place of publication or the publisher is omitted. The date is usually included and is particularly useful in indicating to later readers the relevance of the work, particularly in fast-changing areas.

One other point about the citation of sources in endnotes: when repeated references are made, two useful Latin abbreviations are conventionally employed here – *op. cit.* (*opere citato* – 'the work cited') and *ibid.* (*ibidem* – 'in the same work'). The abbreviation *ibid.* is used when a string of references to the same source follow each other:

Osborne, Brian D: *The Last of the Chiefs*, Glendaruel, 2001, p. 21
ibid. p. 34
ibid. p. 45

and *op. cit.* is used when you refer back to a previously cited document after another source has been cited:

Osborne, Brian D: *The Last of the Chiefs*, Glendaruel, 2001 p. 21
Somers, Hugh J: *The Life and Times of Alexander Macdonell*, Washington DC, 1932, p. 87
Osborne *op. cit.* p. 134
Somers *op. cit.* p. 89

Citations and referencing systems are created to help the reader follow your trail of research; they are also immensely useful in giving later researchers an overview of the sources for your subject. They also will help *you* when, as surely will happen, somebody later asks you a question about your subject and you realise that, with the passing of time, your grasp of everything to do with the subject has slightly slipped – then you will be extremely grateful that you spent time and effort on providing proper references!

Thinking again

As you grow familiar with particular classes of documents you will realise that, very often, much of the content is standard and repetitive and so need not be noted. For example, wills often commence with clauses about the person making the will being of sound mind and body, and being anxious to make proper provision for the distribution of their estate after their death: such standard clauses come from the lawyer's formula book rather than as an expression of the testator's own views, so time can be saved by only recording any significant variations.

As with every aspect of your research you need to keep a questioning mind and an eye open for motive when examining documents. Sometimes the physical condition of the document you are dealing with will suggest questions to you: for example, something purporting to be a contemporary record of events, like a diary, might when you examine it look as if it has been written all at one time – the handwriting is consistent, the ink uniform, the structure shows no sign of stopping and starting or does not reflect the passage of time. This does not necessarily make the document invalid, or even of dubious value – it simply and quite properly raises questions in your mind. Army units in the First World War trenches were ordered to keep War Diaries that were later submitted up the chain of command; did the Commanding Officer actually fill in the official form each day in a muddy dug-out in the front line, or did he scribble down some notes each night and produce a fair copy later when his battalion had been relieved? A diary composed under the first set of circumstances might be quite different in character from one composed in slightly more settled circumstances.

When you have finished making your notes or arranging your photocopying, do not just move on to the next document. Take a moment to stop and think – particularly if you are not likely to be writing up your material immediately. Especially when dealing with manuscript material that may be hard to read, or which presents other problems of interpretation, it is all too easy to concentrate on getting the details of the document and so fail to see the overall picture. A few moments' thought about what the document has told you, what new information you got from it, how far it confirmed or contradicted other documents that you have previously studied, whether it provided the information you expected – and if not, why not – can often pay valuable dividends. Thinking-time is never wasted!

Filing

As you progress in your research you will generate a great deal of material – mostly paper, but perhaps also photographs or computer files. It can become all too easy for information to get lost or for you to spend ages trying to find a missing reference, so from day one you really need to start thinking about how you are going to organise all those notes you take and the photocopies that you will generate.

Because one document may be called upon to provide information for more than one chapter, I find that arranging resources in chapter-based files – while perhaps the obvious answer – is not, in practice, the most useful arrangement. My own method is to get a box file (which will undoubtedly spread to two, three or more boxes as work progresses) and a stack of PVC filing folders (available quite cheaply from any office stationers). I then think about a thematic arrangement and try to consider what sort of information I am likely to collect. This might include topics such as:

- Education
- Marriage
- Children
- Work
- Houses
- Publications
- Obituaries

as well as file titles dictated by the specific nature of the biography I am writing, such as:

- War Service
- Elections
- Travel in Africa
- Meetings with Royal Family

and so on. I stick a list of these folders on the inside of the box file and then arrange the plastic folders in alphabetical order inside. I seldom manage to get the name and number of files right at the start of the project; some topics prove to be very hard to find material on, while others become overloaded and need to be split into sub-topics or otherwise categorised – perhaps by date. This system is only as good as your categorisation, and of course there will always be documents or notes which relate to two or more topics. While it is possible to make multiple copies, you tend in fact to put the document in the topic folder which seems most relevant. The trick is then to remember where you put it: a cross-referencing note in the other folders can be useful.

Even with this fairly systematic approach to organising my information I still spend a great deal of time scrabbling through my files looking for a particular bit of paper. However, it is nothing to the amount of time I would waste if I had not imposed this discipline on myself. A useful by-product of such a thematic arrangement of your documentary resources is that it visibly demonstrates to you the strengths and weaknesses of the evidence you have gathered on various topics or themes.

Chronologies and date-lines

In Chapter 5 I suggested that arranging your narrative chronologically may not always result in the most interesting and convincing story. Despite this you, the author, must have a firm grasp of the chronology of your subject's life. One way of achieving this is to create a comprehensive chronology of all the dateable events and documents in your subject's life. There are many ways of doing this – for example in a card index system, or on a computer database – but I have found that the easiest way is simply to create a document in my word-processing system and lay out a table with columns for year, month and date, a very brief description of the event or document (just enough to jog the memory or identify the event), and the source. The following example, drawn from the chronology I prepared when writing my book *The Last of the Chiefs*, gives an idea of the method:

YEAR	DAY & MONTH	DESCRIPTION OF EVENT OR DOCUMENT	SOURCE
1798		Allan MacDougall, bard to Glengarry publishes *Orain Ghaidhealach*, Edinburgh	Inverness Bibliography
1798	20 Jan	At Holles Street, London. Writes to Henry Dundas on his promotion (purchase of commission)	NAS GD51/6/312
1798	20 Jan	At Holles Street, London. Writes to Henry Dundas on promotion and family arms	NAS GD51/6/312
1798	1 May	Attends meeting of Lieutenancy of Inverness-shire	NAS GD248/193/239

1798	1 May	Attends Ball at Fort George, quarrels with Lieutenant MacLeod over dance with Miss Forbes of Culloden	Scots Magazine
1798	3 May	Fights duel with Lieutenant Norman MacLeod, 42nd Foot	Scots Magazine
1798	5 May	Writes from GGH to Sir James Grant of Grant re militia ballot (ref. to 'my Regiment in Guernsey')	NAS GD248/193/2/16

Some events, like the first one in the sample above, will not be precisely dateable – but others will be.

This method has the great advantage of pulling together information from a wide range of different sources and letting you see them in the same timeframe. It also allows you to make connections that might not otherwise be obvious. For example, in the table above you will see that my subject fought a duel on 3rd May – a fact provided by the trial report in the contemporary press and in the court reports. However, you will also see that by 5th May, he had gone home and was getting on with routine administration. Regardless of whether or not this fact is significant, it is unlikely that I would otherwise ever have associated these two dates because they were provided by different documents at different times and, indeed, were eventually used in different chapters of the book.

When this sort of chronology is well developed it also allows you to identify the periods of your subject's life that are not well documented. There may well be little of interest to say about your subject's life between the ages of 23 and 29, or it may be a vitally important period, but one for which it has proved difficult to find sources. Either way the chronology will graphically demonstrate the peaks and troughs of your research success and can direct your attention to areas where more effort may be needed. As will be emphasised in the next chapter, the whole process of research and writing is a cyclical one and your chronology will grow and evolve as information comes in and is processed and reinterpreted.

8

Writing It Up

You have visited the libraries, consulted the archives, read the books and carried out the interviews – in short, your research is complete and your notebooks, files and computers are full of facts and figures, dates and documents. Now all you have to do is sit down and write it all up.

Well perhaps not quite.

Research and writing may sometimes seem like two separate activities but they are really intimately linked – two parts of the same process. Indeed, there is a research/writing/research/writing cycle which can, if you are not careful, go on for ever. It works something like this:

- You do your research and amass facts and opinions.
- You attempt to write this up.
- You discover in the writing-up phase that there are gaps in your evidence or contradictions in your conclusions.
- You do more research to fill these gaps or resolve these contradictions.
- You return to writing and find that the new information you have gathered informs your opinion on matters you have previously written about, or alters your conclusions on matters you had previously been happy with.
- You go back to do further research to resolve these issues.

And so on, and on... Generally speaking, this circular process is a helpful and constructive one, but be warned; it can go on too long and you can become a perpetual researcher, afraid to commit your findings to paper and communicate them to the world, because there is always another avenue to be explored, another line of enquiry to be followed up. Thoroughness and rigour is all to the good, but libraries and record offices are full of researchers who have never known when to stop.

The condition of being a perpetual researcher is a fairly harmless one, but it does represent a certain loss to the wider community. We research and write for our own satisfaction, certainly, but we should also do it to communicate – and if the researcher never becomes the communicator then we, the wider community, are all the poorer for it. Of course, there is a risk in committing yourself to print; you lay yourself open to criticism, review and comment, and there is no doubt that many people are much more comfortable doing research without having to face the risks of publication. There is also the likelihood that as soon as you go to print, you or someone else will turn up a document of extraordinary interest; publication does have the remarkable tendency to flush out previously unknown documents and, worse still, unknown experts. You should console yourself with the thought that it was to cater for just this type of event that second editions were invented.

The iterative process of research and writing may not be followed by everyone – some lucky, or talented, writers may be so well organised that they can sit down to write as soon as their research is planned and completed. For most of us, though, it is hard to work out in advance exactly what research needs to be done, or indeed what research is possible – particularly if we are writing about somebody who has not been written about before so that there is no 'road map' to show the shape of their life. As we research and write, the need for further research becomes clearer; and with luck, the shape of the life we are working on gradually emerges from the material, rather as a sculpture emerges from a lump of stone.

Planning

With these reservations about the interconnectedness of research and writing, there are some things that still need to be considered under the heading of 'writing up your work'. One issue which has been touched on before, but which bears repetition at this point, is the basic one of planning (see Chapter 5). What is your book or article going to cover? The whole life or just part of the life? How is the work to be internally structured? The decisions that were taken at the outset of your project may well still hold good – but equally the weight of materials that you have found, and perhaps the different levels of interest and relevance within them, might force a reappraisal when you actually sit down to start writing. You know so much more now than you did at the initial planning stage and you need to go where this knowledge takes you. In writing the story of a life you have to be led by the evidence: if the evidence suggests that you should concentrate on one period, where you have good sources and an interesting story to tell, then for your sake, and the sake of your potential readers, you really should follow the evidence and write the story that way. The research and writing cycle will soon show up the areas where your story is thin – and it may well be that there is no way of filling out these thin patches. Better to accept this, acknowledge the problem and play to the strengths of your material than to pad out the thin patches with irrelevancies and unsubstantiated speculation.

Identifying an audience ...

You also need to work out exactly for whom you are writing, at the earliest possible stage. Of course you are writing for yourself and you need to satisfy, and possibly even please, yourself; but you also hope to find a wider audience and you need to give it some thought. It is all too easy to say: 'I am aiming this book at the general reader,' and assume that this is sufficient. But something more precise, even if it is more difficult to define, will help to focus your mind and give you a ready answer when a potential publisher asks (as they will), 'Who is this book aimed at?'

There is probably no such thing as the 'general reader' – rather there is a host of overlapping groups of general readers, all with their own tastes, levels of knowledge and degrees of experience. You want to aim for as wide an audience as possible; even the author of the most *recherché* academic monograph cherishes the hope that an audience outside his narrow professional community will be interested in his work. However, the identification of a target audience in your mind helps you to think through questions of structure, style, language and voice. This audience does not need to be defined by socio-economic theory or mapped by market research: it can be as simple as 'people who enjoyed X's biography of Y' or 'people who watched A's television series on B', or 'people who like visiting historic houses'. Any of these formulations will help to focus your mind on the people who will pick up your book in a library or bookshop, and a focused text with a clear aim and identifiable market is a much better business proposition for your potential publisher than a less structured product – apart from which it is also likely to be a much better book.

... and bringing them 'up to speed'

By this stage in your work you will have become deeply involved in your topic, and intimately familiar with a mass of what will be, to most people, quite obscure events, personalities, organisations and concepts. It is all too easy to make the assumption that everyone else, and especially your potential reader, understands these things just as you do now. You need to think yourself back to your own, earlier level of understanding and remember how you learned all these obscure things. Having done this, you need to try to find a way to bring your reader's knowledge-base up to a level they need to enjoy and use your text – and to do this in as swift, painless and unpatronising a way as possible.

When I was writing my biography of Macdonell of Glengarry I had to deal with his raising a regiment of Fencibles and later a regiment of Militia. Now I knew, or thought I knew, that these were both some sort of reserve army units; and I had some idea that they might have been similar to the Territorial Army or the Home Guard of a later age. But as I read the documents and other books of military history I learned that the Fencible regiments had been raised in the 1790s for full-time military service in a home defence role – so a comparison with the Home Guard was quite inappropriate. Even a comparison with the Territorial Army was not helpful because in the First and Second World Wars, Territorial Army units served alongside regular units in every theatre of operations. The Militia, on the other hand, was much more like the peace-time Territorial Army; members carried on their normal occupations, undertook part-time training, an annual camp and so on, and had the possibility of being called to full-time service only in the event of invasion. So in writing my book it was necessary to explain what both a Fencible regiment and a Militia regiment was to a readership that was probably not going to be any better informed than I had been – and to do so in a way that would not irritate those who were expert in the subject and knew all these facts before they picked up my book.

Finding a style and a voice

You will also need to give some thought to the question of language. How formally do you wish to write? We all tend to speak and write in different registers, and we usually write in a much more formal way than we speak. To take a very basic example, in the previous paragraph I wrote: 'Even the comparison with the Territorial Army was not helpful ...' Had I been speaking these words, even in a fairly formal situation like a lecture, I would probably have said: 'Even the comparison with the Territorial Army wasn't helpful ...' and nobody would have turned a hair. However, I would be very reluctant to use contractions like wasn't, or didn't, or he'll or she'll in print. In part this is because these contractions look ugly and clumsy on the page, and in part because as the result of a traditional education and lifelong exposure to lots of other books, I have an assumption that printed communication should be formal rather than informal. This view is also, undoubtedly, the result of being of a certain age! You may feel that the speed and directness of a more informal kind of communication is appropriate for the work you are writing or the writer that you are; what is important is that you think about the use of language and work out for yourself what style, register and tone you are aiming for and then try to achieve a consistency within it.

Another fundamental issue that needs to be considered is how much of *yourself* you put into your book or article. In autobiography, inevitably, the author is totally on display, but in writing biography a view needs to be taken about the degree to which you will comment or editorialise.

Of course, as we saw when thinking about *Eminent*

105

Victorians in Chapter 1, there is a place for avowedly critical biography, just as there is for enthusiastic advocacy. For most subjects and most authors, who probably have not the skills of a Lytton Strachey, it is nevertheless probably wisest to take a more neutral tone – if for no other reason than the fact that strident condemnation or strident advocacy carries with it the very real risk of arousing contrary views in the reader, who might well come to feel that the subject cannot possibly be as bad or as good as the author is suggesting. There is also the risk that the reader will feel irritated by excessive editorialising and think, probably correctly, that the author does not trust his reader to draw the correct conclusions from the evidence. Denying yourself the luxury of editorial comment does not mean that you have to be without views; and objectivity, as was discussed in Chapter 1, is an illusory goal. You will inevitably shape the book according to your prejudices, and there is no harm in this; but it is probably more effective, and almost certainly more enjoyable for your reader, if you refrain from thrusting these prejudices under their nose at every available opportunity.

Another issue which you will have to address at an early stage in your biographical writing, and one which can sometimes cause a remarkable amount of difficulty, is the very basic one of what you call your subject. The audience you are aiming at will, to some extent, influence your decision on this; for example, a biography for children might take a different approach from an academic monograph. Again, this comes down to a matter of taste – some people writing about the poet Keats might find it perfectly possible to refer to him as John, where others will call him Keats. I would be in the latter camp as I feel that first-name familiarity is somehow inappropriate and disrespectful – although I might take a different view when writing about the poet as a child. There are, however, further complications. To continue in the poetical vein, what happens when you write about William Wordsworth and his sister Dorothy? Do you call him Wordsworth, and if so is his sister, on equal opportunities grounds, also to be referred to as Wordsworth (extremely confusing)? Is she Miss Wordsworth (somewhat old-fashioned), Dorothy (surely rather patronising if William is 'Wordsworth'), Dorothy Wordsworth (long-winded but unambiguous) – or do you engage in circumlocution and use forms such as

'Wordsworth and his sister,' 'the poet's sister Dorothy', which will in any case lay you open to charges of sexism? Needless to say there are no hard-and-fast rules for this sort of decision, and you will probably use a variety of naming formulae in the course of a book. At times, too, there are easy ways out. Take my book about Colonel Alasdair Ranaldson Macdonell of Glengarry: his first Christian name also was commonly used in its anglicised form of Alexander, and he deepened the confusion of nomenclature in later life by deciding to add 'and Clanranald' after Glengarry. To make matters worse, he could also be perfectly properly referred to by his Gaelic chiefly patronymic of Mac Mhic Alasdair. So I was delighted to make use of the Scottish convention whereby a landowner is referred to by the name of his principal property, and was able to save many keystrokes by generally calling my subject Glengarry.

When your work is finished and accepted by a publisher it will be subjected to an in-house editing process, of varying quality and rigour. This should harmonise your text and make it conform to the publisher's house style. Publishers often issue a house-style sheet covering such matters as what to do with full stops (sometimes referred to as points, or full points) in abbreviations like 'Dr' or 'Prof'; or how to handle capitals in cases of personal names and titles. Style sheets also cover such matters as the preferred way of handling dates – should it be:

- 4 March 2002
- 4th March 2002
- March 4 2002
- March 4th 2002
- 4/3/2002, or if you are American, 3/4/2002

To a large extent all these matters of style, and the dozens of others that your publisher's style sheet or one of the published style guides* will cover, are matters of taste. It would be hard to argue that 4 March 2002 is more correct than 4th March 2002: what *is* important is clarity and consistency.

Although your publisher should have your work professionally

*Butcher, Judith: *Copy-editing; the Cambridge Handbook for Editors, Authors and Publishers*, Cambridge University Press, 1992; Ritter, Robert: *The Oxford Guide to Style*, Oxford University Press, 2002

copy-edited, this is sometimes neglected. A perversely treasured possession of mine is a modern book on Scottish history where the same place-name is spelled in three different ways on one page, and elsewhere in it dates are given in successive paragraphs in the forms 24th April 1725 and 24/5/1725.

Even if you are better served by your publishers and their copy-editor than the author of the history book mentioned above (and it would be hard to be worse served), there is no harm in establishing your own style rules and attempting to be as consistent as possible in their application. If you do this, a sensible publisher will probably recognise what you have done and accept your stylistic choices. One publisher I have worked with has the following realistic and helpful introduction to their style sheet: 'This style sheet covers some points of preferred style. In most cases we do not attempt to bring MSS/proofs in line with the conventions listed below if authors have consistently applied their own style throughout.'

In writing biography or autobiography, one of the key stylistic judgements you will have to make is the manner in which you deal with extracts and quoted matter. Some writers tend to précis and reword these, and incorporate them into the body of their writing. This may make for smoother reading, but something of the flavour of the original words may be lost – and the reader will not be able to trace quotations and understand their context. For example, in a report on the opening of the Caledonian Canal in 1823 there was the following comment on the celebrations. These were scheduled to end at midnight, however:

> … some of the gentlemen still remained, and, with genuine Highland spirit, prolonged the festivities of the memorable evening.

It would be possible to incorporate the facts of this quotation into a sentence such as: 'The official celebrations ended at midnight but many of the local gentlemen stayed on and continued the party', but surely the quotation has somewhat more character.

However you decide to handle quotations it is of the greatest importance that you quote accurately and that your sources can be traced – a point we shall return to in Chapter 10. Even a tiny omission from a quotation can totally alter the sense of the extract. Often you cannot, or need not, quote the whole document, but you should do your best to preserve its integrity and avoid editing quotations in such a way that the sense is changed. There is a convention that elision marks (three dots ...) are used to show where matter has been omitted. These can be used at the beginning or end of extracts to show that your quotation has been extracted from a longer sentence:

...enrolled to serve within the Northern Military District...

or they can appear in the middle of a quoted extract to show that material has been left out:

Need I say that ... I refused his demands with contempt.

Care needs to be taken not only to preserve the sense of the original quotation but to also produce an edited quotation that makes grammatical sense and reads well. It is possible – though rather clumsy – to insert a word or phrase, usually enclosed in square brackets, into an edited quotation to render it intelligible or grammatical:

He [the President] said that it was impossible that they [the Japanese] would have known...

If you need to have recourse to this device it might be as well to think whether it would be simpler for the whole quotation to be given, or whether the necessary explanation can be given outside the quotation.

Style sheets will often suggest that extracts and quoted matter should not be displayed in the manner shown above – i.e. with indented margins on both sides, and separated from the text by extra spacing above and below the quote – unless the extract runs to at least five lines; otherwise the extracts should be run on in the text inside single quotation marks. My own view is that in biographical writing, such quotations and extracts are very important and really need to be given the prominence and authority that comes from a displayed setting. While this may make for a rather untidy page, I would argue that the clarity gained by making a strong distinction between quoted matter and the author's commentary, explanation or amplification is worth any possible aesthetic penalty. It is also arguable that when reading a four- or five-line quotation that is run on in the text, and only differentiated by single quotation marks, it can be all too easy to get confused and forget that you are in the middle of a quotation. Finally, displayed setting makes for neater referencing to footnotes or endnotes, as the superscript number – e.g. [17] – simply goes after the last word of the quotation and does not get entangled with the end-quote mark'[17].

In your biography you also need to make decisions about things like weights and measures, and currency. If your subject's rent was paid in pecks of meal, you might feel it appropriate to explain what a peck is. If their annual income in 1785 was £15.6.8 you might feel it necessary to explain to a post-decimalised readership that 6 shillings and 8 pence was 33 pence – and you might also wish to make some attempt to express £15.33 in contemporary values.* Of course, if your subject's income was expressed in foreign currencies, then you will probably need to offer both some sterling equivalent and some contemporary value updating and there are a number of possible sources for this.**

Making a start!

When you have all these stylistic issues and presentational problems sorted out in your mind (although more will assuredly arise in the course of your writing) then you can start putting words on paper. But where to start? Logic might suggest that you begin at Chapter 1, but logic is not always the best guide. Take a look at

---

*A useful source for establishing such values is the website 'How much is that worth today', which enables you to compare the purchasing power of the pound sterling for any year from 1600 with any other year (http://www.eh.net/ehresources/howmuch/poundq.php). This shows, for example, that £15.6.8 in 1785 was equivalent in purchasing power to £1,113.17 today

**Mitchell, Brian Redman: *British Historical Statistics*, Cambridge University Press, 1988; Pick, Franz and Sédillot, René: *All the Monies of the World: a Chronicle of Currency Values*, 2nd ed. New York, Pick Pub. Corp., 1971

the shape of the book you have planned – there will almost certainly be one chapter which is simpler, more self-contained and less problematical, or which is better resourced for materials. If so, this is the best chapter to start with – for a number of reasons.

Firstly, it will do wonders for your confidence to get a chapter under your belt. Secondly, when you come to try to find a publisher or agent – an issue we will think about in Chapter 11 – most will want to see a synopsis and a sample chapter rather than the whole work. Your first completed chapter is thus not only a significant landmark on the way to the finished book, but can be a crucial marketing tool in the struggle to sell your book to a publisher.

Of course, having written this sample chapter months or even years before you write the final chapter has its own difficulties. It means that you need to revise extensively to make sure you do not repeat yourself or assume a knowledge among your readers that they do not yet have. It is here that a good planning document with a fairly detailed breakdown of the contents of each chapter comes in to its own (see also pp. 51–2). If you decide to write Chapter 5 first, for example, as long as you have a reasonably clear idea of the probable contents of each chapter, you can judge what information will have been presented to the reader in Chapters 1 to 4 and avoid repeating it. You also need to make sure that if there *are* any areas of overlap between your first chapter and ones written subsequently, no contradictions have crept in as a result of your increased knowledge and expertise.

Revising and backing-up

One of the great advantages of this computer-dominated age is that text revision is infinitely easier than it was in the days of pen and ink, or typewriter. Not only can you revise and polish your work on a small scale, you can also move great blocks of text around and carry out major revisions and restructuring without the daunting prospect of re-writing or re-typing from the beginning.

If you are using a computer, then it goes without saying that you should be punctilious about backing-up your work and keeping copies on floppy disks or other storage media. Back-up copies should of course also be kept of your research notes and other files that you create in the course of your work; and it would be worthwhile to keep copies of each major revision that you undertake. You might feel entirely happy with the current version of Chapter 7 – but in six months' time new information, or second thoughts about structure, may lead you to conclude that the previous version would now be better. A series of saved files marked 'Chapter 7 version 1', 'Chapter 7 version 2', etc. will enable you to go back with ease, and it is far better to spend a few moments creating these than a great deal of time thinking yourself back to an earlier version, guided only by your memories and what you have currently on file. If you wish to be totally secure, then a second set of saved files stored somewhere remote from your home is a useful insurance. Disasters do happen: I have an author-friend whose house burned down along with all her current work files.

Like many people I find it quite difficult to revise and correct text entirely on screen. It is still simpler and more satisfactory to do this with 'hard copy' – possibly because you can move backwards and forwards in the text more easily, and compare passages and appreciate the overall shape of the piece much better on paper. This means that a very large, and potentially confusing, amount of paper is generated over the course of your writing: it can be very useful to use different-coloured paper for your first or second drafts.

Planning – and finishing - the rest

When you do tackle a particular section or chapter it is tempting to sit down before a blank screen, or a blank sheet of paper, and simply start writing. However, a bit of pre-planning can make for a much more productive process – perhaps incorporating a list of topics to be covered, some indication of how you will link them, a conceptual map of how the various topics to be covered relate to each other or develop one from the other, notes on the sources to be used, and thoughts on the overall shape of the chapter. Some people like making lists and tables; others swear by randomly noting the topics to be dealt with and then linking them with arrows and numbers. How your pre-planning is done is probably less important than the fact of doing it – and of course even the clearest and most detailed chapter plan is likely to be modified in execution. As you start to write you will find that ideas flow in different ways, and that previously unsuspected connections and conclusions come to you. If after thought and testing these seem valid then it is best to go with the flow and not be constrained by the chapter plan you wrote earlier.

However much you chose to depart from the chapter plan, it is essential to return to it again and again to make sure that you are not missing out any essential points. It is all too easy, when the words are flowing freely, to let your fingers run away with you and to find much later that some critical fact has been omitted. Mistakes and misprints are relatively easy to find and rectify; omissions are infinitely more difficult to spot, simply because unless you have a checklist of contents, it is hard to find the fact that is missing, the document that has not been referred to, the important comment that has not been made. This is always irritating but can at times be much worse – for example if you inadvertently omit a reference to a key document or fact in your chain of evidence. Just because you know something 'inside out', don't assume that you have explained it to your audience.

If starting a biography can be problematical, then finishing it is equally difficult. You have tried to avoid being overly judgemental or editorial in the course of the book – but there does come a point at which the author might be expected to reach some conclusions. Of course, you could just stop: perhaps at your subject's death, or at the end of their career, or at another obvious terminating point. Usually, however, some sort of summing-up is needed or at least a passage which puts your subject's life into some sort of context. While it may be undesirable for the authorial view to intrude in the course of the book, it is surely more acceptable for a writer to attempt to pass judgement on their subject in a concluding chapter or passage. After all, if the author has worked well, the reader will now be in possession of the relevant facts about the subject's life and work, views, manners and morals, and can reach an informed conclusion that can be tested against the author's judgement.

If you have written a historical biography, in particular, the final chapter is also an opportunity to refer to what might be called the 'verdict of history' – to look, for example, at your subject's influence on the world, at people's changing views of them, at the way in which other biographers have dealt with them, or to discuss any forms of commemoration of your subject, such as monuments, which might not have readily fitted into the previous text. When I was finishing my biography of Henry Bell I was fortunate enough to be able to use material drawn from the 1912 celebrations of the centenary of Bell's pioneering steamship *Comet*. A couple of pages describing the celebrations in Glasgow and on the River Clyde for this event neatly rounded-off my last chapter, and I felt that they gave the reader a valuable impression of the perceived significance of the man and his work to a generation almost equally remote from Bell's and our own.

James Boswell ended his *Life of Johnson* with a one-paragraph summary description of Johnson's physical appearance, and a very long paragraph outlining his personality and moral character. He prefaced these with a statement that will surely have resonances for other, less famous, biographers:

> The character of SAMUEL JOHNSON has, I trust, been so developed in the course of this work, that they who have honoured it with a perusal, may be considered as well acquainted with him. As, however, it may be expected that I should collect into one view the capital and distinguishing features of this extraordinary man, I shall endeavour to acquit myself of that part of my biographical undertaking, however difficult it may be to do that which many of my readers will do better for themselves.

Boswell concluded his masterpiece with a very unambiguous statement of his view of his friend and mentor:

> Such was SAMUEL JOHNSON, a man whose talents, acquirements, and virtues, were so extraordinary, that the more his character is considered, the more he will be regarded by the present age, and by posterity, with admiration and reverence.

9

Keeping It Legal

There are a number of formalities which you may have to deal with in the course of writing your biography – or to be more exact, in the course of having your biography published, because it is only when you move from private study and research to publication that most of these formalities start to take effect. However it is as well to be aware of these potential problems at an early stage, as you may need to work your way around them or negotiate over potential difficulties caused by them.

Many of these issues are dealt with in an excellent series of booklets published by the Society of Authors, available free to members of the Society and at a very reasonable cost to non-members. For further details you are advised to consult these publications; details of the Society and these booklets appear in Chapter 12.

The necessarily brief information given below is believed to be accurate and is given in good faith – however I am not a lawyer, and it would clearly be wise to take professional advice in case of any doubt or difficulty. One of the many advantages of membership of the Society of Authors and similar organisations is access to advice on matters of contract and other legal issues.

Copyright

At its simplest – and very little in copyright is entirely simple – this is a legal system designed to protect the rights of the creator of a literary or artistic work. It is essentially a property right, but in British law it now also has certain associated moral rights. Copyright exists as soon as a literary or artistic work has achieved 'fixed form' – in other words the *idea* that a book on writing biographies would be a good thing cannot be copyrighted, but this book you are now reading is. In UK law no action needs to be taken to secure copyright; the simple fact of putting words on paper is sufficient to initiate protection. As a result the date of completion of a work may become significant in the event of any dispute over copyright and priority, and some authors take the precaution of sending a copy of their completed work in a sealed envelope by post to themselves, or depositing a copy of the manuscript with a bank and getting a dated receipt.

The symbol © you will observe on the reverse of this book's, and almost every other book's, title page is the copyright notice established by the Universal Copyright Convention and indicates that the work is covered by the appropriate copyright laws of all the contracting states.

The idea of copyright entered British law in 1710, in the reign of Queen Anne, when an act was passed to 'encourage learned men to compose and write useful books'. This phrase is a useful reminder that copyright is a matter of balance, or should be. Balancing, that is, the rights of copyright owners with those of researchers and students; the rights of those who control access to documents or have written books, with those coming after them who wish to write 'useful books'.

A literary or artistic work is any original production in any form created by a human being. Picasso's paintings, Benjamin Britten's operas, Alfred Hitchcock's films, Le Corbusier's architectural designs, John Betjeman's poetry, the novels of George Orwell, the letter your mother wrote to you, and this book are all deemed to be literary or artistic works. There is no test of quality – they need not be 'good' works, but they must be original to come within the scope of copyright protection.

Copyright exists from the moment that the artistic or literary work achieves fixed form, and it extends throughout your life and for 70 years after your death. Until 1996 the term of copyright in the UK was 50 years *post mortem*, but in order to harmonise British and European law a 20-year extension was made. This extension was made retrospectively so that an author who had died in, say, 1925, and whose works had passed out of copyright and into the public domain (that is, available to all to use and reprint without charge or restriction from 1976), was suddenly back in copyright until 2005. There are a number of complications affecting this 'revived copyright' but they are more likely to affect publishers than authors.

The copyright in a literary work, as a commercial property, can be sold, traded or given away, in whole or in part. For example an author may sell stage rights in his work or sell a five-year option to make a film, give his copyright in a work to a charity, or leave it in his will. The copyright in your new biography remains, or should remain, with you the author. The publisher of your book, by agreeing to publish it, gets what is in effect a licence to do so from you – a licence which lapses if, for example, the book goes out of print and the publisher decides not to reprint within a set period of time; in such case the rights to publish revert to you and you can attempt to find another publisher. If your work is a magazine article you will similarly sell rights to publish it in that form but retain the copyright in the article. There has been a recent tendency for some periodical publishers to seek the transfer of copyright from the author – arguing that this makes it easier to sell secondary and subsidiary rights in other media, such as electronic publishing and that the author will benefit from this. Such moves have generally been resisted by authors' organisations. There are exceptional cases where copyright transfer is normal, for example in the case of contributors to a biographical dictionary or a complex multi-authored work where the problems of handling a long list of copyright-holders are obvious. Such cases should be the exception rather than the rule and the general advice must be to retain your copyright.

Facts are not subject to copyright. If you say that a train leaves London Euston at 16:15 for Glasgow Central, Virgin Railways cannot sue you for breach of copyright. You could even print the entire Virgin Railways timetable without breach of copyright – although there is a separate copyright in the typographical arrangement, extending for 25 years from the end of the year of publication, so you could not simply reproduce it.

Although titles are not subject to copyright (see Chapter 5) you may encounter difficulties if, by using a particular title, you appear to be passing your work off as that of another author. It may also be the case that an author has registered as trademarks the title of a work, or the names of characters within it.

The fact that a work is protected by copyright does not stop you making use of part of it: if less than a 'substantial part' is copied then copyright protection does not apply. At the end of Chapter 6 I quoted 32 words from William Dalrymple's *White Mughals* in the firm conviction that this was a less than substantial part of his 600-page book, and my use would be considered 'fair dealing'. Unfortunately there is no precise definition of what a 'substantial part' of a work is or what counts as 'fair dealing'. Certainly both relate to extent and also to significance: 32 words might be an entire poem, or it might be the final recommendation of a technical report, or the concluding paragraph of a detective story, and in each of these cases quoting 32 words could well be considered a breach of copyright. What would certainly be a breach of copyright in even my very limited use of Dalrymple's words would have been to ignore his moral rights – sometimes described as 'the rights of paternity and integrity' – that is, his right to be acknowledged as author of the passage, the right not to have his material attributed to another person or have another person's work attributed to him (the 'paternity' rights), and the right not to have his work altered significantly by addition, deletion or changes (the 'integrity' rights).

There is a specific 'fair dealing' exemption for the use of quotations for the purpose of criticism and review. Having written a biography of, for example, Field Marshal Montgomery, you might wish to end your book by looking at how previous writers dealt with him. There would be no difficulty in quoting a reasonable amount of these other writers' work in order to discuss their treatment of Montgomery – but what is reasonable? Well, there is no hard-and-fast answer to this, and unfortunately it is a very grey area. It is generally accepted that a single extract of 400 words from a prose work would be permissible, or a series of extracts totalling 800 words; by the same token poetry might be quoted in extracts of up to 40 lines, but the extract should not exceed a quarter of the poem. There is also a distinction between quoting for the purpose of criticism and review, and for the purpose of creating an anthology; in the latter case permission needs to be sought for any use, no matter how small.

If your planned use of a quotation or quotations from an in-copyright work is likely to exceed the guidelines suggested above then you can, of course, approach the rights-holder and request permission (see also pp. 121–5). However, asking for permission does not guarantee that you will be given it, or that you will be given it at a cost you can afford. Bear in mind that it is perfectly legal and ethical to summarise, in your own words, another author's work, provided that:

a) you attribute the source;
b) you make it clear that this summary is your interpretation of the other author's work and is not endorsed by the other author;
c) you do not distort the sense of the work.

Some introductory formula such as: 'In my view, Hunter in *Shetland Sagas*[18] is correct in suggesting that the decline in the bardic tradition can be attributed to ...' probably meets these requirements adequately.

It is not always entirely clear who the copyright holder is. For example, if I write a letter to the publisher of this book, then Messrs A & C Black own the physical object, my letter; however I still retain the copyright in it. If a literary work, for example a newspaper article, or a business report written for a commercial company, was created as part of somebody's normal paid employment, then their employer will usually be the copyright owner. However, if the writer of the article is a freelance rather than an employee of the periodical, it is likely that copyright in the article will remain with the author and the newspaper or magazine has only purchased 'first serial rights' – that is, purchased a licence to print the article for the first time. An author can, in theory, sell second, third, and further serial rights, or specific serial rights in different markets – 1st US serial rights, 1st British serial rights, etc. If a work is commissioned – that is, it has been ordered to be created rather than created 'on spec.' and submitted – then copyright is generally held by the author. Commissioned work might well include things like wedding photographs – so the fact that you own a print of your wedding photograph does not mean that you thereby have the right to use that photograph on the cover of your autobiography.

Anonymous works or works that are written by an institution, enjoy copyright protection in the same way as works with a named author or authors, except that the duration of copyright extends for 70 years from the end of the year in which they are published.

There are, you will not be surprised to hear, a number of exceptions to all this.

For a start there is Crown Copyright – the copyright subsisting in official publications. This lasts for 50 years from the date of commercial publication or 125 years from the date of creation of the document. So a report written for the Ministry of Munitions in the First World War, but never commercially published, will remain in copyright well into the 21st century. The text of an Act of Parliament – because it is commercially published – remains in copyright for 50 years, so if you are writing the biography of a politician and wish to print the text of, or quote extensively from, a Private Members Bill he had steered through Parliament, and it is less than 50 years old, you will need to obtain copyright clearance.

There are also three publications which, for various reasons, enjoy perpetual copyright. The Authorised Version of the Holy Bible and the Church of England's Book of Common Prayer are published under letters patent issued by the Crown and so fall outside the normal copyright regime. The third is J M Barrie's *Peter Pan*. Barrie had vested the copyright in this work in Great Ormond Street Hospital and this would, in the normal course of events, have expired in 1987, being 50 years after Barrie's death. In passing the Copyright, Designs & Patents Act 1988 Parliament rather strangely made this one exception and granted perpetual copyright in *Peter Pan* to the hospital. There were, of course, many other examples of copyrights given to charitable causes, but they were not so effectively lobbied for as the *Peter Pan* case. So if you plan to write a biography of J M Barrie and wish to quote from *Peter Pan*, please contact Great Ormond Street Hospital!

The moral rights discussed earlier only apply when a literary work is published in book form; they do not apply to periodicals or, indeed, to work published in dictionaries, encyclopaedias and the like. Moral rights, unlike the property rights in copyright, cannot be sold or assigned – although they can, and usually do, get inherited after death along with the property rights.

There are a variety of other copyright issues which may affect you, including the different treatment of authors from outside the European Economic Area and the treatment of copyright in unpublished works. If you feel that these are going to be relevant, then reference to professional advice or one of the books listed in Chapter 12 might be appropriate.

Note: Copyright law in the UK will be affected by moves taken by the European Community to harmonise intellectual property law, but the broad picture outlined above will probably remain valid.

Permissions

Having established that you need to use a piece of text from another book or a picture, or to reproduce an archival document, the theory of copyright becomes the practicalities of permissions.

The commonest, and often the most expensive, case is obtaining illustrations for your work. Photographic permissions are more troublesome than textual permissions. If you want to reproduce somebody's words, then they either are or are not in copyright. If they are not in copyright then there should be no difficulty in obtaining a photocopy of the relevant bit of the book. If they are in copyright – well, we will come on to that shortly. With illustrations, however, you need to go back to the original source to get a high-quality copy – and it is here that the complications and expense start.

There will generally be two costs involved. Firstly, the reprographic cost – that is, the cost of obtaining a photographic print or a digital image file. This is unlikely to be too expensive, but if you are going to use a lot of pictures you will need to factor it in. The second, the reproduction fee, is potentially a much heavier cost, and is the price of the right to use the photograph or digital file you have just bought. This sum is entirely at the discretion of the owner of the original image and will not necessarily be significantly affected by its copyright status.

Today, nearly all the sources that you are likely to approach for images operate on a commercial or quasi-commercial basis, and will levy as high a charge as they feel they can obtain for the use of their pictures. This cost will vary according to the use that you wish to make of the image, the size of the image, the nature of the book or other publication, the size of the edition and the market into which it is being sold. Thus a picture source might publish a guideline price of, say, £40 per image based on rights to use it in a book published in an edition of 4000 copies or fewer, to be sold in the British market. If the image was wanted for a cover, or world rights were required, then an increased charge would be levied. A larger or smaller print-run would raise or lower the price and the use of a substantial number of images from the same source would normally attract a discount.

Authors are unlikely to know precise details of world rights or print-runs when they first approach a picture source, and picture acquisition is probably best done in stages:

1) Obtain a cheap working copy of all the images that you think you might wish to use. Many picture libraries will respond very helpfully to a request for information and will supply Xerox copies of images in their collection.
2) When you are finalising your manuscript, buy prints or digital-image files of the pictures you are definitely intending to use – and obtain some indication of probable reproduction fees. It is important not to put this off: if you wait until your book is about to be printed you may encounter great difficulties if permission is refused or if the price charged is unreasonably high. Equally, you do not wish to pay a fee for pictures that you do not use.
3) When the book's design has been finalised and you know precisely how many images are being used, where they are being used, and how large an edition is being planned, then you can negotiate reproduction fees.

Despite producing price-lists, picture libraries are frequently open to negotiation on their charges. Some institutions in the public sector will waive or very significantly discount their reproduction fees if they can be persuaded of the educational nature of your project, or its non-commercial nature. Some public bodies (though a diminishing number) view their ownership of original images as a matter of public trust rather than as a source of income, and do not charge reproduction fees; others will waive their published fee in exchange for a copy or copies of the book in which their image appears.

Sourcing images can be difficult, time-consuming and at times puzzling. Recently I had to obtain images of British warships and found that the US Naval Historical Centre was a very much cheaper source than our own Imperial War Museum. Frequently you will find identical images in different collections, all of which will suggest that they own the copyright in the image, when all they actually own is the physical object.

The cost of reproducing two or three images for a biography may not loom large in your considerations – but if you are working on a more heavily illustrated work then you will find that it becomes a major issue. A book I worked on recently had 120 illustrations. My co-author and I eventually agreed terms with one of our major sources, a national newspaper group, for use of their images at £40 each; had we bought all our pictures at this rate our costs would probably have exceeded our likely income from the book! Fortunately we were able to find some lower-cost sources to bring our average cost down to a more affordable level.

It is always worth thinking about alternative, low-cost, sources for illustrations. For example, if your subject is a naval officer and you wish to include a picture of his first command, the probability is that one of the commercial picture libraries will have an image – as may the major newspapers, and almost certainly the Imperial War Museum or the National Maritime Museum. However, the company who built the ship will undoubtedly have taken photographs of it in construction, at launch and on trials and you may well find that they will prove to be helpful, co-operative and cheap.

Turning now to permissions for use of in-copyright text, the first problem is finding the appropriate person to approach. If the work you wish to quote from is currently in print then there is little difficulty. In almost every case, the contract that an author signs with a publisher licenses the publisher to handle the sale of all subsidiary rights, and provides for the sharing of the income from these subsidiary rights between the publisher and the author. Your approach for permission should therefore be made to the publisher, as the author will probably not have the right to agree, independently of the publisher, to let you use his or her work. The author, may, if consulted by the publisher, suggest that no charge be made – after all he or she may be in a similar position some day and may have a natural sympathy for a fellow-author. Indeed the publisher may decide not to make a charge, feeling that the costs and bureaucracy of raising an invoice for a very small sum does not justify the end result.

If the work from which you wish to quote is out of print, but still in copyright, then it is appropriate to approach the author, their representative or their estate. Which is, of course, much easier said than done. The great and the famous are usually quite easily traced – the rest of us can be hard to find. You can try asking the former publisher it they still have a contact address for the author or the author's agent, or contact the publisher of other books by the same author. Standard reference works may also be helpful.

There is an extremely valuable online database run jointly by Reading University and the Harry Ransom Humanities Research Centre of the University of Texas at Austin. WATCH – or Writers, Artists and their Copyright Holders – attempts to provide contact addresses for the literary estates of a wide range of writers and artists whose archives are held in whole or in part in institutional collections in the UK and North America. The WATCH website can be found at http://tyler.hrc.utexas.edu/index.cfm.

There may be circumstances in which the rights-holder for the piece of text you need simply cannot be traced. This is hardly surprising – a writer may have written one book in their mid-40s, never published anything again, and died at 75. The work would remain in copyright for 100 years after the book was written; the rights-holder, who may well not have the slightest idea that they are actually the rights-holder, could be the author's grandchild or great-grandchild.

Assuming they can be traced, there are additional difficulties with what might be called 'amateur rights-holders' – such as the children or grandchildren of the original author. If an author's will has not specifically assigned the rights, they could have been divided among say, three children and may by now have descended to 12 grandchildren. There are obvious problems in obtaining agreement in such circumstances – compounded perhaps by an unreasonable expectation of sudden wealth!

Although it may seem unimportant, the matter of missing or untraceable rights-holders does need to be given some thought. If you use a piece of text without permission it could prove extremely awkward if the rights-holder turns up subsequently. In such circumstances your ability to negotiate an agreed price would be severely compromised – although you could cover yourself to some extent by including a note in the appropriate section of the book stating that every effort had been made to trace the rights-holder, and that appropriate arrangements will be made.

When you have found somebody able to give you permission to reproduce in-copyright material, it is likely – if they are a professional person or company – that they will want to know much the same sort of thing as the picture libraries do: type of publication, the print-run, the market the book is being sold into, the extent of the quotation. Issues may also arise about the integrity of the work: the rights-holder may require assurances that your proposed use of material will not misrepresent the original author's views or be an inappropriate use of the text.

Obtaining and paying for permissions is a matter that should be covered in your contract. Like all contractual matters, this is an area for negotiation with your publisher. A typical contract may make the author responsible for obtaining permissions and paying for them – but it is worth trying to agree on a shared responsibility, at least for costs. In some cases the publisher may also take on the job of obtaining permissions – for example for an anthology – if they think that they may have more success (or more power) in negotiating for them. In some types of publication the cost of permissions is a very major element in the total project cost, and the publisher may wish to handle these in order to maintain budgetary control.

Acknowledgements

Whether or not a fee is charged, you should always make appropriate acknowledgement of the use of all copyright or non-copyright material. While you may not feel that a formal bibliography is appropriate for the type of book or article you are planning, any direct quotations used should be attributed and clearly identified.

It is also normal to express your thanks for any assistance received, in an acknowledgements section; and you might wish to give a copy of the finished book to any particularly helpful people and institutions – for example those who supplied pictures without charging heavy reproduction fees. It is often possible to negotiate an additional supply of free copies from your publisher for just this purpose – a useful way of thanking people at very little cost.

Other legal issues

Your contract with a publisher will undoubtedly contain an alarming clause along the following lines:

Author's Warranty
The Author hereby warrants to the Publisher that the Work is an original work, has not been published in volume form, that he is the sole Author of the Work, that it is in no way an infringement of any existing copyright, that it contains nothing blasphemous, obscene, libellous or otherwise unlawful, that all statements contained therein purporting to be facts are to the best of the Author's knowledge and belief true...

... and so on. This type of clause generally goes on to have the author promise to indemnify the publisher against loss, injury or damage, including legal costs and expenses (as well as the cost of out-of-court settlements advised by the Publisher's legal advisers in order to settle cases).

Quite how often such clauses are enforced is not really the issue; there is a very real danger that what you write will involve you in legal action and potential expense, so it is prudent to consider how best to minimise these risks. Blasphemy and obscenity probably need not detain us too long. Few biographies are likely to arouse these kinds of difficulties and prosecutions for such offences are hardly commonplace nowadays. By contrast, defamation and plagiarism are very real problems for the biographer and writers have famously come unstuck over both.

Your contract will normally be governed by the law of the country in which the publisher is based, and there are significant differences between Scots law and the law of England and Wales. As a very simple example, English law refers to three forms of defamation – criminal libel (a very rare occurrence), civil libel (writing something defamatory) and slander (spoken defamation) – whereas Scots law deals with spoken and written defamation together.

It can be very difficult to define precisely what might be a defamatory statement. The same comment in different contexts may have quite different significance and effect. For somebody to say that I was careless with money might, or might not, be true, but it is unlikely that I would find it defamatory – or, more to the point, that a court would find it defamatory. However, it *could* be a professionally damaging statement to make about a bank manager or a chartered accountant. If your statement can be proved to be true, then that is a complete defence; but in very many cases proving the truth of a statement is very difficult.

In writing biographies, you are writing about real people and need to be careful exactly what you say about them. Obviously you would not wish to say anything that was untrue, but the defence of justification is not an easy one to sustain and if you wish to use it you would need to be sure that every part of your statement was true (and more importantly, could be proved to be true). There is also a defence of fair comment on a matter of public interest – but there is a need to demonstrate that the words complained of were not motivated by malice. And there is a defence of privilege – where a report, which must be accurate and not motivated by malice, of public judicial proceedings can be used in cases where there is a genuine public interest in the matter.

What does all this mean to you as a writer of biographies? Probably that you should take great care to be sure that whatever you say about somebody is fair and accurate; and that if you feel your statements are likely to be controversial, that you take pains to preserve any documents that would support your views. Discuss the matter with your publisher so that they are fully aware of your comments and are supportive of your position.

One comfort is that the laws on defamation only apply to the living, unless your comments on a dead person can be taken to suggest a libel on his or her descendants.

There is the very real danger that writers and publishers are so inhibited by the fear of litigation that they end up saying nothing controversial. It is also true that actions for defamation are expensive and tend to be entered upon by the rich and powerful who can, at times, ensure that little or no public comment on their actions is possible, at least during their lives.

An even more probable cause of difficulties is plagiarism – the unauthorised and unattributed use of other people's material. This can be a legal problem if the unauthorised borrowing is of copyright material and a moral problem in all circumstances.

Of course every author of a research-based work stands on the shoulders of those who have gone before, and it would be impossible and unrealistic to expect every word of a biography to be written without the use of existing texts – it would also make for very bad biographies. Even if your biography is of a subject who has never been written about before you will need to use biographies of contemporaries, histories of the period, and so on, to inform yourself, to fill out the story and contextualise your character. This presents few problems and attributed quotations, as discussed earlier, or citation of works consulted will show your indebtedness and satisfy legal and ethical proprieties.

However there have been notorious cases where authors have been shown to have used, without acknowledgement or attribution, significant passages of another writer's work. In some cases this has resulted in action being taken by the author or publisher of the work from which the passages were taken and expensive consequences have followed, including the withdrawal from sale and destruction of the offending books. Even if the plagiarism is from an out-of-copyright work the damage to the reputation of the plagiarist is likely to be very great.

While there is no reason not to make use of earlier work (clichés about re-inventing the wheel suggest themselves) and existing authors are always very happy to see their work used, referred to and built on, they do, rightly, expect to get credit for their work and are entitled to this degree of respect.

10

Coping With The Technicalities: Illustrations and Index

Illustrating your book

'"What is the use of a book", thought Alice, "without pictures or conversations?"' This question from Lewis Carroll's *Alice's Adventures in Wonderland* is a very valid one: it is hard to think of writing a biography without including some form of visual representation of your subject or perhaps illustrations of people or places associated with them. Some biographies are much more pictorially biased and take on something of the nature of the 'coffee-table book'.

Some of the financial and legal problems of sourcing illustrations were covered in Chapter 9 – here we need look only at the technical requirements, and the issues raised by the range of types of illustration which you may encounter.

You may believe that a large number of full-colour illustrations will enhance your text, but your publisher is likely to feel a very natural degree of concern about the heavy costs of colour reproduction. At an early stage you will need to have reached some sort of understanding about the number and types of illustrations to be included. How many will be black and white, and how many colour; will maps, graphs, tables or diagrams be required and who is going to provide or pay for their provision?

All of these types of illustration can present their own problems. Traditionally, the preferred format for colour and black and white pictures has been as photographic prints or colour transparencies, with a preference for colour transparencies to be shot on a format larger than 35 mm. Colour prints and transparencies can of course also be used to generate black and white (mono) reproductions. Generally speaking, reproduction of an image in a book or magazine involves some degradation of quality – so that the higher quality the original, then the higher quality the reproduction. Photographic prints should be of a reasonable size – 10 x 8 inches or the traditional photographic paper size known as 'whole plate' (8.5 x 6.5 inches) represent a reasonable compromise between quality and economy and are practical both for storage and for posting. Typical 2003 prices from a major picture source for photographic prints are as follows (please note that these prices are for reprographic costs only, and do not include the right to reproduce the image):

- Black and white
  - 8.5 x 6.5 inches   £6.00
  - 10 x 8 inches   £7.15
- Colour
  - 8.5 x 6.5 inches   £12.00
  - 10 x 8 inches   £14.00

Increasingly today, artwork is being supplied digitally and this is convenient, simple and should minimise any degradation of image quality. Your publisher may produce technical guidelines on the format of digital images: for example, these may ask for photographs to be scanned and saved as TIFF images (Tagged Image File Format) at a resolution of 300 dpi (dots per inch). It should be noted that images downloaded from the Internet – which may look acceptable on screen – are usually very low resolution (72 dpi) and will not make satisfactory printed images.

Digital files can be supplied in a variety of formats on 3.5-inch floppy discs, ZIP discs or CD-ROMs. Each image should be saved as a separate file, and a paper print of each should be sent with the material for ease of identification and handling.

Line illustrations such as maps and graphs should also be scanned at high resolution and saved in TIFF format. Remember that line illustrations will often have to be significantly reduced in size to fit on the page, and line weights – or the thickness in which bar lines or lines on a map or chart are created – will be reduced accordingly. For this reason these should start out as at least 1point weight or else there is a very real danger that detail will disappear.

Maps can be very useful in biographies but care needs to be

taken to ensure that copyright held by, for example, the Ordnance Survey is not infringed by basing a map on Ordnance Survey data. If you need to get maps or other graphics prepared for your book, do ensure that the cartographer or graphic artist has a very precise brief which, for maps, should include a list of essential locations that must be included and some indication of the relative size and significance of these locations. Many specially drawn maps prove to be less than useful because the artist has not fully understood the background to the project or has failed to include the essential information.

It may be that some types of information about your subject can best be conveyed by graphs or charts, and these are now easily produced on computer. However, do bear in mind that the fancy pattern and coloured fills that your computer program can produce will not reproduce well in black and white. Tints for computer-generated illustrations should not be too dark or too light – something in the range of 15% to 70% works best.

It is very useful to the designer of the book if you can indicate the ideal positioning of each picture or other illustration. To some extent positioning has always to be a compromise, but the author's views on where an illustration might best be placed should be available to the designer.

The index

When your text is complete you will need to think about an index – something which should be included in any biography or other serious work that you hope may have some long-term reference use. Indexes are important and useful and deserve to be given proper attention.

There are freelance indexers available who can quickly and efficiently index your text. There is a great deal to be said for employing a professional indexer who has the training and experience to be able to look at your work objectively and see it from the perspective of the reader. An indexer will certainly not know the subject-matter of your book in the detailed and thorough way that you now do, but this freshness of vision can be extremely helpful. Your eventual readers will, after all, be in a similar position and will have to extract information from your book without having the advantage of your detailed knowledge.

Creating an index is not cheap, but it is an investment in the value of your finished book. In 2003 the Society of Indexers (contact details in Chapter 12) recommends rates of between £1.50 and £5.00 per page, or £16.00 and £30.00 an hour depending on the level of complexity of the text, the length of the book and index, any time constraints imposed, the experience of the indexer and other factors. A list of indexers and their specialisations is available from the Society.

If you are going to prepare your own index then you will need to give some thought to its nature and extent, and to what you want it to achieve. Standard word-processing packages like Microsoft Word have index creation programs: these allow you to mark up your text so that index entries are created for specified words and for more general concepts, and also allow for the use of cross-referencing. It is important to consider what search terms, or 'headwords' as they are often called, your reader will use when searching for information. These may be very specific, such as:

Reid, Alan: birth 24
Reid, Alan: attends Albert Road Primary School 27, 29–30

though some entries will be much more general and relate to concepts, movements, and ideas rather than to concrete, specific places and events. The precise word chosen as the search term may not actually appear in that form anywhere on the printed page – such as:

Reid, Alan: political views 123, 134, 178, 186

Some of your index entries will be very simple while others will require multi-level, nested entries. It is generally considered good practice to avoid sub-sub-entries – so :

Reid, Alan
   Aviator   123–9
   Merchant Banker 234–6
   Politician   56–7, 123–45, 157–9, 182–4
   Novelist   212–13, 234

is acceptable, but

Reid, Alan	
Politician	
Conservative	56–7
Liberal Democrat	123–45, 157–9
Socialist Workers Party	182–4

becomes confusing and increasingly hard to read.

The largest concentration of index entries will of course be for the subject of your biography, and these need to be arranged in some sort of order – either as an alphabetical list of topics or as a chronologically arranged list of topics.

There are a number of conventions for the presentation of page references. For example, 61 is a single reference; 61, 62 indicates two separate references; and 61–2 indicates a continuous reference spanning both pages. It is normal to elide page references – thus 223–6 rather than 223–226, although numbers in the teens normally retain two figures for clarity and appearance – thus 117–19 rather than 117–9.

It is all too easy to over-index – to include every occurrence of a headword, even where it is merely mentioned and adds nothing new to the sum of the reader's knowledge. This can be extremely irritating to the user, who sees a list of index entries such as:

Ark Royal HMS	56–7, 70, 74, 86, 92

and finds that two or three of these entries are created simply because the ship is named on that page and no useful information is given. Index entries are much better created sparingly and with some thought to practicality and the end-user's benefit, rather than on an unselective basis of 'let's put it in just in case it might be useful' or, even worse, 'let's make the index as long and as impressive as possible'.

You should also give some thought to cross-references. There are two sorts of cross-reference: the 'see' reference and the 'see-also' reference. See references are used to direct readers from unused terms to preferred terms, e.g. Bowmen <u>see</u> Archers. However, if a particular term occurs only once or twice it is probably just as easy to duplicate the entry and include the non-preferred term, rather than send the reader from Bowmen to Archers only to find one page reference. See-also references are used to direct readers to related terms, e.g. Lake Poets <u>see also</u> Coleridge and Wordsworth.

Although the page numbers for your index cannot be finalised until the final proof stage has been reached – because pagination is not known at manuscript stage and may change from first proofs – if there are many corrections and alterations, you should prepare a list of headwords when your final manuscript is submitted. The publisher will need to allow the appropriate amount of space for the index when planning the book; and although the page references for each headword may take up several lines, the list of headwords will give a fairly good indication of the probable extent of the final index. In any case, the presence of a great many page references for particular headwords is a useful indication that these entries could be broken down. You might find that you can create multi-level entries and give any obvious, discrete elements their own sub-headings.

11

Getting Published

The last word has been written, the last reference checked, and the whole book or article spell-checked, grammar-checked and read over and over again. It is as good as you can make it – now to get it published!

Some of this comes down to basic common sense. Most books on writing will give you the same advice and, no matter how much you may want to be different, there is every reason to conform. I am sure that if an author has written a work of transcendent genius it will be published, even if it is handwritten on small sheets of green paper in purple ink and bound in antique vellum. However, it is extremely unlikely that either you or I will write a work of transcendent genius, so we need to give ourselves every chance.

Preparing your manuscript for submission

Your manuscript should be:

- Typed or word-processed in a clear and legible typeface. Although they are not so commonly found nowadays, avoid using dot-matrix printers which, when set to economy mode, produce a thin grey text which is very hard to read. You want the editor or whoever reads your text to enjoy it – not to develop eyestrain and an irrational dislike of your work.
- Text should be double-spaced. Yes, it is expensive in terms of both paper and postage, but it gives room for editorial changes and is easier to read.
- Text should not be justified. Your computer-justified text probably does looks neater, but it is said to be easier to calculate space with unjustified text.

- Text should be printed on one side of white A4 paper (or if you are in the US, on letter paper which is marginally larger).
- Do not bind or staple your pages. For a magazine article, clip them together with a paperclip; for a book-length manuscript find a box or a long elastic band.
- Do make sure that your pages are numbered, either continuously from 1 to the end or starting a new sequence for each chapter.
- Put a running head at the top of the page so that if your typescript gets mixed up in the office it will be possible to identify it. If you are giving a new sequence of page numbers to each chapter, ensure that your chapter name or number is included in the header.

If, as may well be the case, your manuscript is not accepted by the first, or the second, or the tenth publisher you send it to, do ensure when it goes out to the eleventh that it still looks fresh and clean – consider reprinting the first few pages. It does nothing to help your cause if a publisher realises that your manuscript has been rejected several times before.

Finding the right publisher

This can be difficult – and if you are an unknown, with no track record of publication, proposing a biography of somebody else who is less than well known, it can be *very* difficult. There is little doubt that the odds are against you – a very tiny proportion of speculative submissions to publishers are ever actually commissioned. This is doubtless unfair but it is hardly surprising: if you were a publisher and had two manuscripts on your desk, one by a known author with whom you had worked before, and the other arrived in this morning's post from somebody you had never heard of, which would you rather invest your time and money in? How then can you, as a first-time author, break in?

First of all by aiming at the right target. Find out who publishes the type of book or article you have written or are writing. There are several ways of doing this – the simplest is to look on library and bookshop shelves and see who publishes similar titles. You could ask for advice from a librarian or a bookseller.

You could also consult one of the books like *Writers' & Artists' Yearbook* or *The Writer's Handbook* that list book and magazine publishers and their areas of interest. The entries in these books will also usually include some indication of how the publisher would like to be approached: 'Initial enquiry before submission of mss,' 'Synopses with sample chapter and table of contents,' 'No unsolicited mss; synopses and ideas welcome.' Unfortunately there is absolutely no standardisation in this field – one magazine will suggest phoning the Editor, while another insists on written submissions with stamped addressed envelope for return. This might be confusing but there is no real alternative to complying with the individual publisher's or journal's requirements. You want to give yourself as good an opportunity of success as possible, and annoying the commissioning editor is not a good first step.

The proposal

You can further help your chances by putting together a persuasive package. Many publishers and agents will not consider a complete typescript as a speculative submission – it takes far too long to read, and an assessment of its merits can be made on a much smaller sample. More effective by far is to prepare, possibly at quite an early stage in your research and writing, a really compelling proposal that can be sent to publishers along with a sample chapter. This proposal should be designed to convince the publisher that your book or article:

- will make them money;
- will satisfy a public demand;
- will be an appropriate title for their list, or content for their periodical.

It should also convince them that you:

- are the appropriate person to write it;
- can deliver the goods.

The proposal is not an area in which your natural modesty and diffidence can be allowed to hold sway. Without being dishonest or over-selling yourself, you need to make a clear and persuasive case for why, in the first instance, the hard-pressed editor should invest time in reading your work, and why, thereafter, anyone will want to pay good money to read it.

A strong proposal will:

- Be short – a couple of sides of A4 at most. If you manage to intrigue or interest the editor, they can always ask for more details.
- Be positive in tone and commercially aware. Publishers are inevitably and properly commercially driven. Projects that seem to have little or no chance of making money are hardly likely to prosper. If you indicate that your book will have a very limited market and needs 120 colour illustrations to do it justice, you may find a certain lack of enthusiasm.
- Explain exactly who the subject of your biography is, why they are worth writing about, and why anybody would want to read about them. Do not assume that everybody will know.
- Indicate what other books exist on the subject and why yours is different, or better, or needed. What is your book's 'unique selling proposition'? Is it the first book on the subject? Have you found some new and important sources? Is there a need for a reappraisal of the subject? Is there some external reason why a new life is appropriate – such as a centenary in a year or so? Have you some specific insight you can bring to the book?
- Provide some information about you and your qualifications to write the book. Explain your interest in the subject, what attracted you to them, your qualifications to write about them – which does not just mean that you have an Honours Degree in Modern History, but could mean that you came from the subject's hometown, are her grand-daughter, lived in his house, have had a life-long interest in him, found a bundle of her letters in a junk-shop. Explain also what, if anything, you have written before.

Spend time on the proposal. Polish and refine it. Cut it down to the essentials. Aim for a confident, competent, persuasive tone that will make the editor think that if they reject you they may be missing out on something big. It is your prime selling tool, and as the old adage says, you never get a second chance to make a first impression.

The long wait

Having got your package together – covering letter or proposal, synopsis, contents listing, sample chapter – then send it off, with the traditional stamped addressed envelope for return. Do try to find out to whom you should be addressing the package – it is much more professional to address any correspondence to a specific member of staff rather than just to the company. Many publishers include the names of their commissioning editors in works like *Writers' & Artists' Year Book*. If they do not provide this, then a phone call to the company should produce a contact.

Having done everything right and sent off a powerful, effective proposal package, all you can do is wait. It can take some publishers a very long time to reject a proposal – others do it almost instantly. It is hard to decide which approach is worse: a long delay allows the author to think that the proposal is being minutely and carefully considered at the highest level, while an instantaneous rejection brings with it the conviction that nobody really looked at it. The sad fact is that the success rate for unsolicited proposals – for works that come from what publishers inelegantly but descriptively call the 'slush pile' – is frighteningly low. By low I mean 1 or 2%. Which may provoke the thought, 'Why bother?' Well, if what you are writing is something that you believe in – that you feel needs to be written, and you are the person to write it – then you *will* bother. My own first biography – which I naturally took all my own advice about – spent a couple of years going round 19 different publishers before eventually finding a home with what was then a very new and small publisher. Persistence pays off, sometimes.

It is worth remembering that there may be many very good reasons why even the best, most interesting, well-targeted and attractive proposal is rejected. The publisher may have a financial crisis and be cutting back; they may be re-shaping their list so that your proposal does not suit the company's future plans; they may have just commissioned another book on a very similar topic; they may know of a competitive work that is in production for another house. Any or all of these and other reasons can make your proposal unsuited for that publisher at that time.

Authors' agents

One more certain way to attract a publisher's interest is for your manuscript to come to them from a literary agent. Agents have the great advantage of being closer to the fast-changing publishing scene than you can be; they will be aware of much of the internal politics outlined in the previous paragraph and will know where and when to submit your work. If your work comes endorsed by an agent that the publisher knows and respects, then this acts as some guarantee of quality to the publisher. While it will not ensure acceptance it will elevate your manuscript from the 'slush pile' to more rapid, and perhaps more thorough, editorial consideration.

However (and as always there is a 'however'), it is by no means an easy task to get a literary agent to take on a new client, especially an unknown first author. Agents live by their share of the author's royalties – usually taking 10 or 15% of royalties and subsidiary income. The ideal client is therefore an author who will write regularly, sell well, and whose works offer lucrative opportunities for the sale of subsidiary rights like newspaper serialisation, film and TV adaptation. Someone who might turn out to be a 'one-off' writer of a minority-interest book, selling into a limited niche market, is hardly likely to represent an attractive business proposition to an agent. A very simple calculation will confirm the reasons that lie behind the agent's doubts:

Total sales of book: 2000 copies
Cover price: £10.00
Royalty to author: 8%
Author's gross income: £1600
Agent's income at 15% of author's gross: £240

£240 is not a lot of money on which to run a business, to spend time reading manuscripts, to spend time persuading a publisher to read a manuscript, to negotiate a contract, etc. So while agents are undoubtedly highly beneficial, it can be just as difficult to get an agent interested in you and your work as it is a publisher. It becomes easier to get an agent when you are established and have a track record, but even so, many of the best-known and most prestigious agencies note in their entries in *Writers' & Artists' Year Book* that their client lists are full.

Despite all these counsels of despair, books do get published – a great many of them each year, well over 100,000 titles in the UK alone. There is no reason why yours should not form part of this tidal wave. So keep on trying.

The publishing contract

When your book is accepted you will receive a contract from your publisher and will be asked to sign and return a copy as soon as possible. Despite your natural delight at having got to this stage, it is worth reading this document very carefully. Remember that the contract document is a basis for negotiation between the author and the publisher, not Holy Writ that must be accepted without question. The financial terms you are offered may be fairly standard but should be read with care. Exactly what are you being offered?

The traditional way to express authors' royalties was as a percentage of the (fixed) retail price. This was generally around 10% on hardbacks and 8% on paperbacks. Several things have happened to produce a move away from this simple system. Retail price maintenance on books was abolished in 1997 and the cover price is now a recommended price rather than a guaranteed fixed price. Bookshops, particularly the large chains, have become more aggressive in their demand for margins and the former trade norm of 35% discount has crept up to 40, 45, 50% and above. Many publishers now express authors' royalties as a percentage of net receipts. This is a perfectly reasonable way of working but it should be noted that the percentage rate needs to be considerably higher than the 8–10% level to compensate for the changed basis of calculation. A £10.00 book with royalties at 10% on the percentage of retail price basis will produce royalties of £1.00. The same book sold to the book trade at, say, an average discount of 40% will produce receipts to the publisher of £6.00; so to produce the same level of income for the author, the percentage of net receipts rate needs to be 16.6%.

Your contract will probably also include a clause covering what are described as 'high discount sales' – that is, sales where the publisher has been obliged to give a discount in excess of 50% to wholesalers and large retail groups. In such cases the royalty rate is reduced, perhaps to as little as 10% of net receipts. Such sales are hardly good news for the author – our notional £10.00 book sold at, say, 52% discount will produce a £4.80 net income for the publisher (who of course has to pay warehousing, distribution and representation costs in addition to the costs of book production and marketing as well as business overheads and the author's royalties) and £0.48 for the author.

Quite apart from the royalty terms being offered, there are a number of other potentially contentious issues which are worth noting, for example the division of the income from subsidiary rights, the arrangements for the reversion of the rights to the author if the work goes out of print (a much more difficult concept in the age of 'print on demand'), and of course the vexed question of an advance. Contracts generally make provision for the payment of an advance against royalties, perhaps payable in three stages – on signing of the contract, on delivery of an acceptable manuscript, and on publication. The size of the advance will of course be determined by many factors: the size of the edition, the price, the possibility of subsidiary rights sales and the keenness of the publisher to secure your book. This last element usually only comes into place with best-selling novelists and authors of sensational memoirs, when advances of telephone number dimensions are sometimes achieved. Sadly neither the author nor the typical reader of this book is likely to be in this category! The advance should represent a reasonable percentage, say two-thirds, of the likely earnings from the first print-run of your book.

The Society of Authors (contact details in Chapter 12) produces a useful Quick Guide to Publishing Contracts available for £10.00 to non-members. The Society also offers members an invaluable contract-checking service.

Revisions and proofing

Once your book has been accepted there may be a request for revision from the publisher. Do not be too precious about this – it may be the first time your work has been seen by a dispassionate outsider. If the editor suggests a change, there is probably a good reason for it: think about the areas where changes are being suggested and try to see why they are being asked for. The editor will work with you in making changes and getting the overall shape of the book right.

After this desirable stage has been reached, your work will go through a process of copy-editing and, with luck, all the little inconsistencies and inaccuracies, stylistic quirks and spelling mistakes that you have let slip will be caught. At this stage your text will also be marked up for typesetting. Authors have been known to have the odd grumble about copy-editors who try to rewrite their work on grounds of taste and style, replacing the authorial voice with their own; or about copy-editors introducing errors into texts, like the copy–editor who changed an author's spelling of cannon (a large piece of artillery) to canon (an ecclesiastical dignitary) with comic results (King James II of Scotland was thus killed by an exploding priest). However, most copy-editors do a valuable and necessary job and their changes should always be treated with respect – if cautious respect.

The last stage for the author before seeing the finished book is checking the proofs. This is *not* the stage to have major second thoughts and decide that 500 words should come out of Chapter 3 and into Chapter 5. You will probably find a clause in your contract which says that other than for printer's errors, author corrections which cost more than 10% of the cost of composition will be charged back to the author. This does not mean that you can change 10% of the proofs without cost. The costs of correction, being more complex work – finding the correct place, working out what the correction is, making the correction, reformatting the text, etc. – are much more expensive than straightforward typesetting.

Checking proofs is time-consuming and very hard work: there is a natural tendency to see what you know should be on the page, rather than what actually is. There is no substitute for close, line-by-line, word-by-word scrutiny of the text and probably for two or more complete readings.

Selling it

The book has been written, the contract signed, proofs checked and the finished book sent to the printers – but your work is not over yet. Selling the book is primarily the publisher's business but it is an area in which the author can be of considerable assistance. You may not be a household name who will be booked for TV appearances and national author tours, but you do have contacts who can be used to help promote your book. Your publisher should take steps to gather this sort of information from you – but if they fail to do so, there is nothing to stop you supplying them with it anyway. You may be a member of a society whose other members would be interested in your book, or you may have a local reputation which can be exploited by a display or signing session in your local bookshop or a talk in your local library. You will undoubtedly know of specialist journals, organisations, libraries, etc. devoted to the subject of your biography which can be targeted by your publisher. You may have come across some distinguished authority in the course of your research who would be prepared to endorse your book, write a foreword, or provide a suitably glowing quote for the jacket. All of these areas of special-ist knowledge are, or should be, at your fingertips. Your publish-er's publicity person will not have the specialist contacts and insights that you have, so it is important to work with them to make a success of the promotion and sales of your book.

You also need to be willing to get out and get your hands dirty – to be available for launches, signing sessions, radio inter-views, or whatever. Local radio will often pick up on newly published books with a local connection and want to interview the author. This may be nerve-racking the first time round but it is worth doing. Just be prepared to talk and keep on talking about the things that you want to get over – sometimes you even get to submit in advance a list of questions. Even if this doesn't happen it is useful to have thought about some of the likely questions and practised some answers, and like all interviewees the more experienced you get, the easier it is to answer the question you want to talk about rather than the question the interviewer actually asked. Do not expect your interviewer to have read your book with detailed care and attention – if they have read your publisher's information sheet that may be as much as you can expect! Remember too that your interview may be severely cut to fit the space available, so if you can, try to provide a pithy sound-bite about the book that can get the message across – and make sure that your name, the book's title and the publisher are clearly communicated.

It is well worthwhile trying to produce a 40–50 minute presentation on the subject of your book and making it known to likely organisations that you are available and willing to talk. Not only should this provide a fee, however modest, but it also provides you with a splendid opportunity to sell your book direct to the public. Your publisher should have made arrangements for you to buy your book at trade terms and the prospect of making 35% or 40% profit on sales after a talk is some inducement to travel to a draughty church hall on a winter evening. One suggestion: if you are giving a talk and selling books, advise the organisation in advance that books will be available for sale. It is remarkable how many people come out to meetings without money!

PLR

Once your book is published you should register it with the Public Lending Right Registrar (contact details in Chapter 12). This requires completion of a simple form, and for your first registration the form needs to be countersigned by an independent witness who is not a relation and who has known you for two years. Once your book has been registered, and assuming that any copies of it find their way into libraries and are borrowed, a small sum (currently 4.85p per loan) will be paid to your bank account each year. PLR will never make you rich, and there is a capping limit so that extremely successful writers do not scoop the pot, but it is a welcome addition to your income. The annual statement makes interesting reading and, if you have several books registered, provokes reflections on why title A seems to be much more successful than title B.

Other options

If all your best efforts to find a publisher fail, then there are a number of possible avenues open to you.

- Recycle your book into another format. Can you produce some magazine articles from it, or adapt it for radio or the stage?
- Pay somebody to publish it. We discussed vanity publishing or subsidy publishing in Chapter 1, and it is an option – if not one that can normally be recommended.
- Publish it yourself. Again touched on in Chapter 1. A risky but possibly rewarding option. Have you the time, energy, persistence and self-belief to go around bookshops and other outlets persuading them that they want to buy your book, negotiating discounts, arranging sale-or-return terms, and coping with rejection – which is particularly hard when it is your book, your pride and joy, that is being rejected? If you have, and if you have a handy space in which to store 2000 unsold copies of your book, by all means go ahead and think about it. You will be in good company – some established authors who have found, perhaps as a result of changes in editorial personnel or corporate structures, that their work was no longer wanted by their publishers have gone down the self-publishing route with considerable success. Others have found their garage occupied by parcels of books for a very long time.
- Web publishing. As we saw in Chapter 1, this gives everybody the low-cost route to publishing. If you really want your book to be available to the public and do not care whether you make any money from it, then this is a very interesting and increasingly used avenue – and one that offers you total control over the appearance and contents of the finished product.

Whatever route you end up taking to publication, and whatever struggles you have along the way, I am sure that you will find the process satisfying and rewarding – even if your reward comes in the thrill of seeing your work in print and knowing that you have added to the sum of human knowledge rather than in a huge royalty cheque. Good luck!

12

Useful Addresses

Libraries and archives

Bodleian Library *
Admissions Office, Clarendon Building, Broad Street,
Oxford OX1 3BG
Tel: +44 (0)1865 277180
Fax: +44 (0)1865 277105
Email: admissions@bodley.ox.ac.uk
Web: www.bodley.ox.ac.uk/guides/admisfrm.htm
Catalogue: www.bodley.ox.ac.uk/elec-res.html

British Library *
Reader Admissions, 96 Euston Road, London NW1 2DB
Tel: +44 (0)20 7412 7677
Fax: +44 (0)20 7412 7794
Email: reader-admissions@bl.uk
Catalogue: blpc.bl.uk

British Library Newspaper Library
Colindale Avenue, London NW9 5HE
Tel: +44 (0)20 7412 7353
Email: newpaper@bl.uk
Catalogue: www.bl.uk/catalogues/newspapers.html

Cambridge University Library *
West Road, Cambridge CB3 9DR
Tel: +44 (0)1223 333000
Fax: +44 (0)1223 333160
Email: library@lib.cam.ac.uk
Admissions: admission@lib.cam.ac.uk
Catalogue: ul-newton.lib.cam.ac.uk/

Commonwealth War Graves Commission
2 Marlow Road, Maidenhead, Berkshire SL6 7DX
Tel: +44 (0)1628 634221
Fax: +44 (0)1628 771208
Email: casualty.enq@cwgc.org
Web (Debt of Honour register of war dead): www.cwgc.org/

Family Records Centre
1 Myddleton Street, Islington, London EC1R 1U
Tel: +44 (0)870 243 7788 (Birth, Marriage & Death Certificates)
    +44 (0)20 8392 5300 (General enquiries)
Email: certificate.services@ons.gov.uk
    enquiry@national.archives.gov.uk
Web: www.familyrecords.gov.uk/frc

General Register Office for Scotland
New Register House, Edinburgh EH1 3YT
Tel: +44 (0)31 334 0380
Email: records@gro-scotland.gov.uk
Web: www.gro-scotland.gov.uk

Greater London Record Office
London Metropolitan Archives
Greater London Record Office & History Library
40 Northampton Road, London EC1R 0HB
Tel: +44 (0)20 7332 3820
Fax: +44 (0)20 7833 9136
Email: ask.lma@corpoflondon.gov.uk
Web: www.corpoflondon.gov.uk/lma

Imperial War Museum
Lambeth Road, London SE1 6HZ
Tel: +44 (0)20 7416 5320
Email: mail@iwm.org.uk
Web: www.iwm.org.uk/lambeth/index.htm

National Archives of Ireland/An Chartlann Náisiúnta
Bishop Street, Dublin 8, Ireland
Tel: +353 (1) 407 2300
Fax: +353 (1) 407 2333
Email: mail@nationalarchives.ie
Website: www.nationalarchives.ie

National Archives of Scotland
Historical Search Room, General Register House,
2 Princes Street, Edinburgh EH1 3YY
Tel: +44 0(131) 535 1334
Fax: +44 0(131) 535 1328
Email: enquiries@nas.gov.uk
Web: www.nas.gov.uk/

National Army Museum
Royal Hospital Road, Chelsea, London SW3 4HT
Tel: +44 (0)20 7730 0717
Email: info@national-army-museum.ac.uk
Web: www.national-army-museum.ac.uk/

National Library of Scotland *
George IV Bridge, Edinburgh EH1 1EW
Tel: +44 (0)131 226 4531
Fax: +44 (0)131 622 4803
Email: enquiries@nls.uk
Web: www.nls.uk
Catalogue: www.nls.uk/catalogues/index/html

National Library of Wales *
Llyfregell Genedlaethol Cymru *
Aberystwyth, Ceredigion SY23 3BU
Tel: +44 (0)1970 632 800
Fax: +44 (0)1970 615 709
Email: holi@llgc.org.uk
Web: www.llgc.org.uk
Catalogue: www.llgc.org.uk/cronfa/index_s.htm

National Maritime Museum
Park Row, Greenwich, London SE10 9NF
Tel: +44 (0)20 8858 4422
Fax: +44 (0)20 8312 6632
Email: No enquiries by email
Web: www.nmm.ac.uk

National Monuments Record
Great Western Village, Kemble Drive,
Swindon SN2 2GZ
Tel: +44 (0)1793 414600
Fax: +44 (0)1793 414606
Email: nmrinfo@english-heritage.org.uk
Web: www.english-heritage.org.uk

National Portrait Gallery
St Martin's Place, London WC2H OHE
Tel: +44 (0)20 7306 0055
Email: archiveenquiry@npg.org.uk
Web: www.npg.org.uk

National War Museum of Scotland
Edinburgh Castle, Edinburgh EH1 2NG
Tel: +44 (0)131 225 7534
Fax: +44 (0)131 225 3848

Probate Search Room
Principal Registry of the Family Division
42–49 High Holborn, London WC1V 6NP
Tel: +44 (0)20 7947 6000

Public Record Office/The National Archives
Kew, Richmond, Surrey TW9 4DU
Tel: +44 (0)20 8876 3444
Fax: +44 (0)20 8392 5286
Email: enquiry@nationalarchives.gov.uk
Web: www.pro.gov.uk
Catalogue: www.pro.gov.uk/catalogues/default.htm
Online access to PRO Information Leaflets:
    www.pro.gov.uk/leaflets/riindex.asp

Public Records Office of Northern Ireland (PRONI)
66 Balmoral Avenue, Belfast BT9 6NY
Tel: +44 (0)28 9025 5905
Fax: +44 (0)28 9025 5999
Email: proni@dcalni.gov.uk
Web: http://proni.nics.gov.uk

Royal Air Force Museum
Grahame Park Way, London NW9 5LL
Tel: +44 (0)20 8205 2266
Email: hendon@rafmuseum.org
Web: www.rafmuseum.org.uk

Royal Commission on Ancient and Historical Monuments of Scotland (RCAHMS)

John Sinclair House, 16 Bernard Terrace, Edinburgh EH8 9NX
Tel: +44 (0)131 662 1456
Fax: +44 (0)131 662 1499
Email: nmrs@rcahms.gov.uk
Web: www.rcahms.gov.uk
CANMORE database: www.rcahms.gov.uk/canmoreintro.html

Science Museum Library

Imperial College Road, South Kensington, London SW7 5NH
Tel: +44 (0)20 7942 4242
Fax: +44 (0)20 7942 4243
Email: smlinfo@nmsi.ac.uk
Web: www.sciencemuseum.org.uk/library/index.asp
Catalogue: www.sciencemuseum.org.uk/library/smlcats.asp

Scottish National Portrait Gallery

1 Queen Street, Edinburgh EH2 1JD
Tel: +44 (0)131 624 6200
Fax: +44 (0)131 343 3250
Email: pginfo@nationalgalleries.org
Email: portrait.archive@nationalgalleries.org

Trinity College Library, Dublin *

College Street, Dublin 2, Ireland
Tel: (+353 1) 677 2941
Fax: (+353 1) 671 9003
Email: No email address listed
Web: www.tcd.ie/Library/
Catalogue: www.tcd.ie/Library/Catalogue/

The above libraries and archives all have their own access arrangements and restrictions – details of which can usually be found on their websites. As a general rule, access for serious enquirers should not be overly restrictive especially if you can demonstrate that the materials you are seeking are not readily found elsewhere.

The libraries marked with an asterisk have legal deposit privileges and are entitled to a copy of every book published in the

United Kingdom and Republic of Ireland.

In addition to the above, most University libraries will have some arrangement for access to their collections for *bona fide* researchers, either on a reference-only basis or with lending facilities. A preliminary approach to the University Librarian, indicating the nature of your proposed research, will be helpful.

The major public libraries in cities such as Birmingham, Edinburgh, Glasgow, Leeds, Liverpool and Manchester have extensive reference collections of great research value and all public library systems have significant local studies collections. Details of such collections can be found in the works noted in Chapter 6.

Useful organisations

Church of Jesus Christ of Latter-Day Saints (Mormon Church)
The Distribution Centre, 399 Garretts Green Lane,
Birmingham B33 0UH
Telephone Sales: +44 (0)8 700 10 20 51
Fax Sales Line: +44 (0)8 700 10 20 52

This centre distributes in the British Isles the CD-ROMS of the 1881 British Census and the British Isles Vital Records Index.

Public Lending Right Registrar
Public Lending Right, Richard House, Sorbonne Close,
Stockton-on-Tees TS17 6DA
Tel: +44 (0)1642 604699
Fax: +44 (0)1642 615641
Email: authorservices@plr.uk.com
Web: www.plr.uk.com

The Society of Authors
84 Drayton Gardens, London SW10 9SB
Tel: +44 (0)20 7373 6642
Fax: +44 (0)20 7373 5768
Email: info@societyofauthors.org
Web: www.societyofauthors.org

The Society publishes the following guides available to non-members at the prices indicated (current at the time of writing):

Quick Guides £10.00 each post-free:
  Bringing a Small Claim in the County Court
  Electronic Publishing Contracts
  Ghost Writing/Collaboration Contracts
  Indexing Your Book
  Publishing Contracts
Quick Guides £2.00 each post-free:
  Authors' Agents
  Copyright and Moral Rights
  Copyright in Artistic Works Including Photographs
  Income Tax
  Libel
  Literary Translations
  Marketing Your Book
  Permissions
  The Protection of Titles
  VAT
  Your Copyrights After Your Death
Occasional Papers £1.00 each post-free to non-members:
  Film Options on Literary Properties
  Multi-Author Projects
  Packaged Books and Co-Editions
  Revised Editions
  Vanity and Self-Publishing

The Society of Indexers
  Blades Enterprise Centre, John Street, Sheffield S2 4SU
  Tel: +44 (0)114 292 2350
  Fax: +44 (0)114 292 2351
  Email: admin@indexers.org.uk
  Web: www.socind.demon.co.uk

The Writers Guild of Great Britain
  15 Britannia Street, London WC1X 9JN
  Tel: +44 (0)20 7833 0777
  Fax: +44 (0)20 7833 4777
  Email: admin@writersguild.org.uk
  Web: www.writersguild.org.uk

Index